A selection of *Indian*

Vegetarian recipes from

Hansa's *Award Winning*

Gujarati Restaurant

"I dedicate this book to
all of my family, *friends*
and *customers* who have *helped,*
supported and *guided me*
from the very beginning, to make
my dreams come true.
And a *special mention* to
Kokila Parmar *(everyone's Masi)*
who has stood by me from

the very beginning"

Hansa Dabhi

❧ Foreword

I consider myself very honoured to have been asked to provide the foreword for this fascinating book. Having visited Hansa and eaten at the restaurant of the same name, I am well aware that the beautifully photographed dishes in this volume do taste just as good as they look! I did think however that the book could not do justice to the ambience created at the establishment but I have been proven wrong. Packed with information about the origins of dishes and with helpful hints on the health-giving properties of ingredients, this book is more than just a collection of recipes, it is a journey through a culture. Hansa's origins as outlined in the introduction on page 8 and the rather romantic tale of her and Kish's elopement certainly give credence to the maxim : *"triumph through adversity".* However, being very generous of spirit Hansa has decided to let her readers experience all the triumph with none of the hardship, which is also very much our motto here at the Vegetarian Society. We know that there are many reasons why people become vegetarian and it is our job to make it easier for them to do so. Food such as Hansa's make it not only easy but extremely pleasurable. With a few more books and restaurants such as this we could all be happily redundant!

Enjoy and experiment.

Tina Fox
Chief Executive, Vegetarian Society UK.

Hansa's Indian Vegetarian Cookbook

First published in Great Britain in 2000 by Hansa's Publications.

PO Box 204

Leeds LS17 8WJ

England

Author: Hansa Dabhi

Publisher: Kishor Dabhi

Assistant Editors: Alan and Linda Brown

Art Director: Amanda Chauhan

Photography: Sue Hiscoe

Printed by: Art Printing Works, Malaysia

Hansa's Restaurant, 72/74 North Street Leeds LS2 7PN

www.hansasrestaurant.co.uk

ISBN: 09538326

❦ Contents

Foreword   5

Introduction   8

About this book   12

Eating Gujarati style   16

Notes   18

Utensils   20

Spices   22

Set menus   24

Starters   26

Chutneys   40

Specialities   46

Main courses   56

Beans & pulses   68

Rice & sauces   78

Breads   94

Salads, raitas & pickles   104

Desserts   114

Drinks   126

Leftovers   132

Medicinal properties   134

Glossary   136

Suppliers   138

Index   140

The Ugandan Asians who fled to Britain from the wrath of Idi Amin in

1971 have had a remarkable effect on the commercial and cultural life of their adopted country. Amongst their number was a fifteen year-old girl, then called Hariganga Mistry, and her family One of six children of a Gujarati worker in the sugar mills at Kakira, childhood years gave her little preparation for life in Yorkshire; autumn and winter in Leeds were a far cry from the 'green and pleasant land where the sun always shines' that she remembered from her school geography lessons. However, a background that combined influences from India, East Africa and the West Riding has shaped the style of cooking that she developed, first in her home and then in her popular restaurant, Hansa's.

Custom dictated that, as well as attending school, all of the children, especially the girls, had to do the household chores. As the youngest daughter, Hansa's were the most menial. The rebel spirit, so evident later in her life, caused her to object when her sisters were given the more responsible tasks. At school in Uganda most lessons were conducted in English with some in French, Swahili and Gujarati, Hansa's mother tongue. On moving to England she experienced few problems in adapting to a different educational system, once she had got used to the Yorkshire accent and the embarrassment of being called 'love' by strangers.

After leaving college at sixteen a different phase of education began for Hansa. She started work as a VDU operator for the Post Office and had to deal with the demands of adults who needed immediate responses – again good training for her future career. At this time, she also started to get to know other girls of her own age but from different backgrounds. Their interest in boys, going out and dressing up were far removed from her own strict, traditional upbringing. A normal day for Hansa meant preparing breakfast for the family before work, cooking an evening meal on her return and then helping to clear up afterwards. Her main memory of any extra free time was that it was spent huddled round a gas heater watching TV. The week's main outings were a shopping expedition on Saturday and a visit to the Hindu Temple on Sunday.

In 1978 a major change occurred. Hansa met Kishor and started to see him regularly and in secret. Her strict parents, members of the Kumbhaar caste (the potters and joiners) would never approve a union with Kish whose family were from the Mochi (or

Hansa, staff and family at the opening of Hansa's.

shoemakers) caste. And so, after a secret and, to western ears, rather romantic elopement, Hansa and Kish were married against her parents' wishes.

This sudden break from the shackles imposed by the expectations of parents, in-laws and the community, left Hansa and Kish feeling liberated. They started to make decisions for themselves, becoming more daring as time went on. Kish became a lecturer in Engineering in 1979 and one year later they became parents when their son Manesh was born, to be joined by a second son, Anand in 1982. Hansa spent much time with local playgroups and the NCT (National Childbirth Trust) and was always in demand for Indian cookery demonstrations and food stalls at fund-raising events. The skills she had learned from her mother and mother-in law, combined with her own flair and enthusiasm, were a popular combination; the idea of using them as the foundation for a

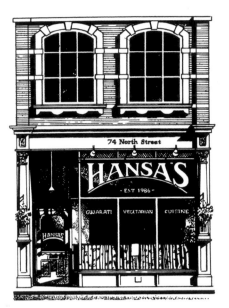

career took root and, on her thirtieth birthday, bore fruit as her restaurant was opened.

The opening of Hansa's, by Kapil Dev, India's World-Cup winning cricket captain was the culmination of a sustained effort. Encouraged by friends, Hansa had prepared thoroughly. Neither she nor Kish had a background in business or catering so she took a range of courses to prepare herself, persuaded a bank manager to agree to a loan and mortgaged their house as security.

Equally important was the development of a guiding philosophy. There were to be three basic principles. It was not to be a 'veggie cafè' but a fully-fledged restaurant serving pure vegetarian food. At the time this was a daring step; the image of vegetarians in this country was not positive, as can be seen in the popular TV series of the time, 'The Young Ones'.

Secondly, Hansa was determined to abolish the myth that most Indians live on a meat diet. The menu was to be different from that offered by most Indian restaurants. You will search in vain for Chicken Tikka Masala, Meat Vindaloo or Prawn Madras in Hansa's. What you will find is much better!

Thirdly, the dishes offered would be like those enjoyed every day by the average Gujarati family. Most customers had to be guided through the menu at first. Many, like me, found the menu informative and so interesting that they could be seen reading it long after orders had been placed. The emphasis is on home cooking; the homely feel is also evident in the warm welcome and open approach of all the staff. The food is cooked and served by women, as is normally the case in Asian households. It is not always strictly traditional though; I had tasted one of Hansa's chutneys many times before she told me that the two main ingredients are tomato ketchup and mint sauce. Another unusual item, sliced white bread, appears in her own creation, Pau Bhajiyas. Most of the dishes, though, would be familiar to Indian families and all are faithful to the spirit and traditions of Hindu vegetarian cookery.

Hansa and Kish are always happy to talk about Hindu customs and beliefs. Festivals

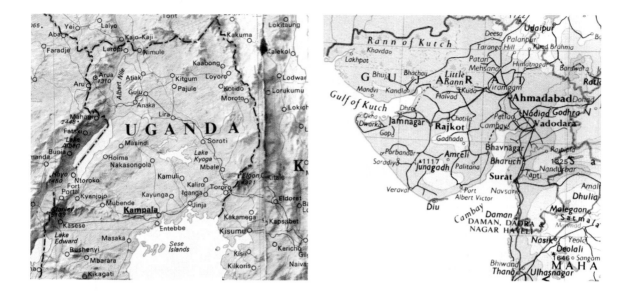

such as Diwali are observed with seasonal menus and traditional dishes and the various rites and rituals explained. They, in turn, are interested in the religious practices of others. Very few restaurants can claim to increase understanding between people of different faiths but it is a natural consequence of the approach in the early years of the business.

In the Hindu culture to be a vegetarian is regarded as a virtue, eating the flesh of dead animals is seen as a lowly existence. The common western view, that only meat can provide the full range of vitamins, proteins and minerals, is disproved by the numbers of vegetarians in India (about 720 million) who, like generations before them, have fit, healthy and active lives. Hansa's food, though, is the best advertisement for vegetarian food that I know. Look at the pictures in this book. Try the food, either cooked by yourself at home or by Hansa. If you can, meet Hansa and talk to her about what goes into one of her dishes. She will tell you that there are no difficult techniques involved and will be happy to give you advice. Gujarati food must be one of the best-kept secrets in the west. The recipes in this book are an excellent introduction.

Alan Brown

Customer, fan and friend.

" It is *not* a
problem but a
pleasure to be a
vegetarian in
this *beautiful*
world of ours "

Hansa Dabhi

About This Book

This book is the culmination of my experiences and growth as a cook. It contains recipes of dishes enjoyed by my Gujarati family on a daily basis, modified to suit the taste of my customers. The state of Gujarat is situated on the West Coast of India (see map page 11) where my parents originated. It is a predominantly vegetarian state whose inhabitants are renowned in the rest of India for their delicate style of cooking. Our food is slightly sweeter than in other areas and uses a subtle blend of spices. The flavour of the vegetables and pulses is enhanced and the absence of oily curry sauces means that lighter dishes are produced.

The Hindu scriptures of India, the Vedas, emphasise the fact that *'you become what you eat'* and that controlling your diet is the key to controlling your bodily functions and your physical and psychological well-being. A whole scripture is devoted to this holistic approach to the use of vegetables, pulses and spices in promoting good health and spirit in man.

The recipes in this book also contain useful hints and tips about the use of certain vegetables and spices to alleviate some common ailments, ranging from simple headaches to problems suffered during pregnancy. For this information I am indebted to my mentor, Dr Surendra Sharma, the advisor to the Indian Government on Ayurvedic Medicine. Ayurveda, the science of promoting longer life, is a branch of medicine with a long tradition rooted in Hindu scriptures, written some 5000 years ago. For millions in India it forms the basis of their primary health care, using as it does, only natural products to treat everyday problems. Expensive modern medicines with their side effects are used as a last resort.

The contents of this book draw together my experiences as a Hindu living as a vegetarian in the West. My Indian, East African and English upbringing all influence the recipes and the choice of ingredients, producing dishes that are a little different and reflect my individual tastes. I hope that you will enjoy the results of my culinary journey to date and that they will provide you with an experience that is both physically and mentally satisfying.

"It is not a problem but a pleasure to be a vegetarian in this beautiful world of ours."

Hansa Dabhi

Hansa's (front row second from left) humble beginnings in Fort Portal (Uganda) 1963.

❀ Eating Gujarati Style

In India we do not have formal courses like starters, mains and desserts, instead everything is served at the same time and people eat it all together, taking more, or less, of whatever they like during the course of the meal.

I have been asked many times by my customers how to eat our Gujarati meals and my reply has always been that most Indians use their right hand when eating a meal and derive great pleasure from it. Obviously washing your hands before and after a meal is essential. We tend to eat the curries with breads first then move on to eating the rice with the remaining curry or daal sauce. The way you tackle a meal will depend upon what you are eating.

Most of the starters are fairly easy to eat using fingers. We tend to break up the starters, one at a time, into small bite-size pieces and then dip each piece in the sauce or scoop a little chutney with it and pop it into the mouth quickly, before any of the sauce or chutney dribbles off on to your fingers or into your lap.

The Masala Dhosa is quite tricky. In India the Dhosa (pancake) is enormous with only a little filling in the middle. The reason for this is that you use the unfilled portion of the Dhosa as you would use chappatis, i.e. break off a small piece and use that to squeeze a little of the masala (filling) and scoop it up together with the sauce (sambhar) and the coconut chutney and eat it, a little at a time. Consequently, by the time you arrive at the middle portion, only a small amount of masala will be left to finish off, without making a mess.

The Masala Dhosa I serve in my restaurant is much smaller but filled throughout its length with the mixed vegetable masala. I myself prefer it that way and so do my customers. They tend to eat it with knives and forks, pouring both the sauce and the chutney, a teaspoonful at a time, and eat it as they would eat most other meals.

Sometimes customers would complain that they found the curry too hot and spicy. On my questioning as to how they ate the curry I would find out that they used the fork to scoop up the curry and eat it, followed by rice or chappatis. Therein lies the problem. The curry is always eaten by scooping it with a piece of chappati or some rice. It is usually too spicy to eat on its own. The breads and rices help to dilute the spicy taste to acceptable levels.

When eating curries with chappatis or any other Indian breads, break a small piece, about 2 inches square, place it on top of the curry, at the edge rather than the middle, and scoop up enough curry to fill the bread and pop it into your mouth. In this way your fingers should remain fairly clean at all times. Practice makes perfect.

When you have had enough bread then take some rice. First mix it with the remaining curry or pour some daal or kadhi sauce on it and make a small bite-sized mound. Pick up the mound using all your fingers if necessary and pop it into the mouth quickly. Alternatively, a spoon or a fork could be used.

A little dab at the pickles and dessert keeps all the taste buds activated with a host of flavours throughout the meal.

We Indians lick the fingers clean after a meal and wash the hands after.

A little dab at the pickles and dessert keeps all the taste buds activated

 # Notes

Indians tend to use sunflower oil or vegetable oil for all of their cooking and frying. Olive oil tends to change the taste of the food since it has its own flavours, depending upon the country of its origin.

To get the best results from the recipes mentioned in this book and save time please follow these suggestions:

Familiarise yourself first with the requirements of the recipe by reading it thoroughly. All the measurements are both in imperial and metric equivalents (ie lb/oz to kg/gms, pts to l/mls, etc. The metric measurements have been rounded off to avoid complicated numbers.)

> 1lb = 16ozs = 450gm – weight measure used
> 1 pint = 560ml – liquid measure used

Allow extra time when attempting unfamiliar or complicated recipes. The cooking times mentioned are a good guide for the person who is quite confident with Indian cooking.

Assemble all the ingredients necessary and prepare them as suggested, i.e. measured, chopped or ground, etc. before commencing the cooking process. This will give you confidence that you are not leaving out any essential ingredient in a rush to complete the cooking process.

Gas hobs tend to heat up faster than electric hobs so the cooking times mentioned should be used as a guide only. Some experimentation is required to suit individual appliances.

❧ Utensils

Throughout the whole of this book I have tended to use the basic utensils that you would find in most ordinary kitchens just to give heart to the uninitiated, so that they are not bewildered by the complicated sounding names and shapes of the utensils used by an Indian cook. However, as you gain confidence and familiarity you may wish to purchase the equipment mentioned in this chapter.

Masala Tin - The stainless steel spice-tin, a perfect birthday present to ask for. Every Asian household will have a masala tin which makes life so much easier since it contains as many as 10 little stainless steel tins, neatly arranged within a 10-12 inches (25-30 cm) round tin with an air-tight lid. All the dry spices you need for cooking an Indian meal are stored in here, so that cooking can commence immediately. The spices have a fairly long shelf life generally but they are kept fresh in this tin for a longer time, which makes a lot of sense since they are fairly expensive. It also helps you to keep a tab on the spices as they run out and replenish them as necessary.

Tavi (or Tava) - This is a shallow but heavy cast iron or steel griddle about 8-12 inches (20-30 cm) in diameter, slightly concave in the middle, used for making most baked breads. Some Asian shops also sell these griddles made out of clay, but these do not have a handle so a pair of steel tongs, known as Saansi, are necessary for handling them. As to which is better is all up to personal choice. The steel griddles are more versatile in the long run.

Velan (Belan) - This is an Indian rolling pin. Unlike the western cylindrical rolling pin the velan is tapered on both sides which facilitates the application of gentle pressure more precisely to the chappatis or puris.

Patlo - The circular wooden rolling surface for rolling the Indian breads is usually bought together with the velan. The normal size is around 8-10 inches (20-25 cm) in diameter. The modern kitchen worktop forms a very good alternative.

Karai - Now a familiar item in all Balti Houses, the Karai is a larger version of the deep circular bowl-shaped steel utensil, used for deep frying all the fritters and the puris. The Karai comes in various sizes, depending upon the quantity of frying one does, but for an average household of four a 12inch (30 cm) diameter Karai should be quite adequate. The only problem with a Karai is that it requires a special steel ring, also available from the Asian shops, which acts as a stand for its concave base, to stabalise it when sitting it on the gas or electric hob. Many Asian households prefer to use a thick aluminium basin instead, since it has a flat bottom and therefore sits perfectly on a gas or electric hob and the aluminium does not rust.

Tapelas - The Indian cooking pans tend to be mainly high-sided aluminium pots, with a $^{1}/_{2}$inch (12mm) rim. They come complete with a flat cover. It is thought that these seal the steam better than the normal pans, but that is debatable. You buy them in a set of four in descending sizes from 12inches down to 6inches (30cm-15cm) and use them depending upon the quantities required. The whole set fit snugly inside one another to reduce space. The normal thick aluminium pans would be good enough for most of your needs.

Pressure Cookers - A pressure cooker is a very useful utensil for boiling beans and pulses since it can reduce cooking time by up to seventy percent.

🌼 Mari-Masala - Spices

Indian cooking cannot exist without spices. The Ayurvedic approach dictates that spices should be used sparingly to enhance the taste of the vegetables and the pulses as well as promote the physical wellbeing of the individual. There is a tendency in the West of demanding the use of extra spices in order to make the curry very potent, with the obvious effects on the gastric and the digestive systems. Stomach ulcers and heartburn are the two most common immediate effects on the body any such over-indulgences. Chillies used in small quantities are known to alleviate arthritic pains but can also cause stomach ulcers and gastric problems when taken in larger quantities. I have included many such medicinal tips throughout the book to bring this point home.

The list of spices is endless but I have restricted myself to the use of spices that are easily available in the local Asian grocery shops and supermarkets. Most of the spices nowadays are cleaned and packaged to a very high standard and it always pays to try out the spices blended by different manufacturers until you find the one that gives you the best results.

The content of my masala tin (spice-tin) are as follows:
Turmeric (hardar) powder, red chilli powder (lal marcha-ni bhukhi), cumin and coriander mixture (dhanna-jeeru), garam masala, salt (nimakh), mustard seeds (rai), cumin seeds (jeeru), carom seeds (ajmo), fenugreek seeds (methi), cloves (laving), cinnamon (taaj), cardamon (elchi) and dried red chillies(sukha lal marcha).

Fresh green spices include ginger, garlic and green chillies. They are best prepared as the cooking begins although they can also be prepared and frozen in an ice-tray and used a cube at a time as required.

The herbs most commonly used in my cooking are coriander, fenugreek and dill.

Chilli powder *(marcha-ni-bhukhi):* This is available in two strengths, hot and extra hot, so use it according to your personal preference. The quantities I have used would make a mild curry but please do experiment until you achieve the taste that you like.

Cumin seeds *(jeeru):* These are brownish seeds with a likeness to caraway seeds. Cumin seeds are used in vegetable and rice dishes to give them a rich aromatic flavour. Dry roasted cumin seeds, coarsely ground or crushed, give raitas and lassis a very special taste.

Cumin and coriander powder (dhanna-jeeru): This is available ready mixed or they can be bought separately. I prefer to mix my own, in equal quantities, as I find that the ready mixed ones tend not to be equally balanced.

Turmeric (hardar): This is a yellow powder used mainly to give the curries the distinctive rich yellow colour. It must be used in very small quantities to avoid overpowering the curry with its strong bitter after taste. Turmeric, especially when mixed with oil, will easily stain the work surfaces and clothing so avoid spilling it or handling it with bare hands.

Garam masala: Garam masala, meaning hot mixture, is a mixture of at least ten different spices mixed in varying quantities. Every Gujarati household has its own recipe for making garam masala to suit their own taste. Mine will remain a closely-guarded secret but my garam masala will be available on request. You can also purchase it ready mixed from most Asian grocery shops.

The garam masala can be used at the cooking stage or as a garnish. It tends to change the colour of the curry to a darker shade so use it sparingly. Daals and pulses benefit the most from garam masala as they tend to be rather bland in taste.

Mustard seeds (rai): These tiny purplish brown seeds have a very powerful bitter taste and a small quantity of the seeds is used to flavour the curry by first sizzling them in some hot oil until they pop and then mixing the rest of the ingredients in it. This process is known as 'waghaar'.

Mustard seeds are mainly used with vegetable curries and certain dry daal curries.

Carom seeds (ajmo): These tiny brown seeds are a member of the cumin family. Flavoursome carom seeds are sizzled in hot oil before adding certain beans to it, such as vaal and black eyed beans, to ease the digestion of these beans.

Fenugreek seeds (methi): These are tiny mustard coloured seeds with a very bitter taste. They can be used whole or crushed. The whole seeds must be sizzled in hot oil before adding the vegetables or daals to it or can be used crushed for pickles.

Cloves (laving): This pretty looking spice almost resembles a tiny flower but has a very strong aromatic flavour. I tend to use it whole to flavour some rice dishes, kadhi and daal sauces and the garam masala of course.

Cinnamon (taj): The bark of the cinnamon tree has a slightly sweet aromatic taste and is used like the cloves to flavour the rice dishes and the vegan desserts such as lapsi and sev. It is also one of the main ingredient of the chai masala (spicy tea mixture).

Cardamon (elchi): Cardamon comes in green, white or black pods. The seeds of the green and the white pods are used to enhance the flavour of rice dishes, some hot desserts and some pulses. The seeds of these pods are crushed or ground and used as a garnish for most of the Indian desserts.

The larger black cardamon is used as one of the ingredients of the garam masala.

❦ Set menus

I know how difficult it is to plan a menu, especially when you do not know or cannot remember what each dish tastes like and whether they complement each other. I have listed four suggested menus for you to choose from, just to get you started and give you confidence with your future adventures with my various recipes. These combinations are what my customers have enjoyed the most and I'm sure you will enjoy them too, but please do not let this make you feel tied down, since there are no hard and fast rules as to which dish goes with what. The essence of my cooking has always been that you should cook what you personally enjoy the most and mix in something different for variety. This is what makes cooking such fun for me!

Menu Suggestion 1

Starter
Kachoris with tomato and mint chutney - p29

Main Course
Posho and Maag Daal curry with puris, plain rice, tuwer daal and onion and tomato salad - p55

Dessert
Sev - (Vermicelli with milk) - p118

Menu Suggestion 2

Starter
Patra with tamarind and date chutney - p32

Main Course
Ondhiyu and Chora and Mushroom curry with baturas, pilau rice, raita and kadhi - p50

Dessert
Shrikand - p117

Menu Suggestion 3

Starter
Pau Bhajiya with coriander and mint chutney - p26

Main Course
Bhaji and Chevti Daal with rotli, pilau rice, sambharo and kadhi - p57

Dessert
Gulab Jambu - p113

Menu Suggestion 4

Starter
Dhokhra with coconut chutney - p31

Main Course
Ravaiya and Garam Masala Daal with baturas, Jeera rice and onion and tomato salad - p59

Dessert
Gajjar Halwa with cream or plain ice-cream - p115

No Gujarati meal is ever complete without a crunchy, spicy papad (papadom)
to give that added taste

Pictured clockwise from top left: Posho, Patra, Gajjar Halwa and Pau Bhajiya.

Carom seeds -
ajmo are good
for *indigestion*

Mustard seeds - rai
are used for *skin disorders*

Starters and snacks

Pau Bhajiyas   29

Bhajiya   30

Kachori   33

Petis   34

Dhokhra   35

Patra   36

Makai-no-Chcvdo   39

There are no such things as starters in a Gujarati household where their dishes can be eaten as Nashto (meaning breakfast), or snacks between meals. All starter-like dishes are served along with the main meal as a side dish or at tea time or as a breakfast snack, depending on the type of snack and the time of day.

These snacks are made from almost anything and everything, e.g. daals, vegetables, rice and breads. Some are specially made, whereas some are simply made from leftovers.

Most Indian women have a great talent for creating and inventing such dishes which are then passed onto friends and family when they come to visit.

A karai or a wok or a deep fat-fryer and a slotted spoon are the essential utensils when making these starters.

Serve with a *chutney* of your choice

🌸 Pau Bhajiya My own East/West creation

SERVES 6

PREPARATION TIME 60 MINS   COOKING TIME 25 MINS

1lb (450gm) potatoes *(boiled & mashed)*
4oz (100gm) peanuts *(coarsely crushed)*
4oz (100gm) sweetcorn kernels *(frozen)*
2 tbsp sesame seeds
1½ tsp green chillies *(crushed)*
½ tsp cinnamon powder
1 small onion *(finely chopped)*
10 sprigs fresh coriander *(finely chopped)*

1lb (450gm) gram flour
Juice of ½ lemon
6 slices thin or medium bread *(cut into 24 triangles)*
Oil for deep-frying
2½ tsp salt
½ pt (280ml) water
1 tsp sugar

method for filling
Heat 2 tbsp of oil in a pan, add sesame seeds, cover the pan and remove from the heat. Add the sweetcorn, peanuts, salt and green chillies, mix well and let it cook on low heat for 10 mins and then let the mixture cool down.

When cool, add the mixture to the mashed potatoes with fresh coriander, chopped onions, sugar, cinnamon powder, lemon juice and mix well.

Spread a layer of mixture about ½in (10mm) deep on all of the bread triangles.

method for the batter and frying the bhajiyas
Add water to the gram flour and 1½ tsp salt and mix well.

Heat the oil for deep frying to a moderate heat.

Keeping the triangle flat, dip into the batter and gently slide it into the oil. Fry a few at a time, turning them over to make sure the batter is cooked on both sides.

Remove with slotted spoon and place them on a paper towel to soak up the excess oil.

They are now ready to be served with the chutney of your choice. Tomato and mint chutney is my favourite.

🐾 Bhajiyas Extremely popular Indian fritters & easy to make

SERVES 4-6

PREPARATION TIME 10 MINS   COOKING TIME 15 MINS

½lb (225gm) gram flour *(sifted)*

2 tsp chilli powder

3 tsp dried fenugreek leaves or ½ bunch of fresh fenugreek leaves *(finely chopped)*

5 sprigs fresh coriander *(finely chopped)*

2 tbsp lemon juice

1lb (450gm) fresh vegetables of your choice (or mixed variety): potatoes, onions, cauliflower, courgettes, aubergines, mushrooms, banana, and chillies *(thinly sliced)*

Oil for deep-frying

1½ tsp salt

Water

method

Add all the ingredients (except for the vegetables) in a bowl and gradually add water to form a batter. Continue to mix by hand. The consistency should resemble that of a cake mixture, maybe slightly thinner.

frying

Heat the oil to a moderate heat in a wok or deep-fat fryer. Dip the vegetables in the batter, one at a time, and drop gently into the hot oil. Repeat quickly until the pan is covered. Turn over the bhajiyas until both sides are golden brown.

Remove with a slotted spoon onto a paper towel.

Serve hot with the chutney of your choice (see chutneys section).

Tip: *If your fritters are too oily, turn up the temperature of the oil.*

Coriander - dhania
is *good* for
headaches
and *indigestion*

fenugreek leaves -
methi are
useful for
diabetes and
joint pains

🦁 Kachori A classical Gujarati snack

SERVES 6

PREPARATION TIME 60 MINS   COOKING TIME 90 MINS

Stuffing:
8oz (225gm) frozen peas
4oz (112gm) mung daal
1 tsp green chillies
1 tsp ginger *(crushed)*
1 tsp garlic *(crushed)*
Juice of ½ lemon
10 sultanas
½ tsp cinnamon powder

4 sprigs fresh coriander
1½ tsp sugar
1 tsp salt

Pastry:
2½ oz (70gm) plain flour
2 tbsp oil
½ tsp salt
3 tbsp water

method for stuffing
Coarsely grind the soaked daal and peas together in a food processor.

Heat 4 tbsp of oil in a pan, add the ground daal, peas, ginger, green chillies and salt. Mix well and let it cook on a low heat stirring frequently until the daal is soft.

Remove from heat and add sultanas. When the mixture is cool add sugar, cinnamon powder, coriander and lemon juice. Mix well. The mixture should be firm enough to form balls. If the mixture is too dry then add a little oil. Form into 12 balls.

method for dough
Blend the flour with ½ tsp salt in a mixing bowl. Add 2 tbsp of oil and rub in well using fingertips.

Add cold water gradually to form firm dough. Knead well with a little oil. Form into 12 portions.

forming the kachoris
Take a ball of dough and roll it out into a 4 inch (100mm) circle. Place a portion of stuffing mixture in the centre. Bring the sides of dough over the filling to enclose securely.

Twist the excess dough from the top and break it off. With the centre of your palms shape the pastry into a ball shape. Continue to do this with the rest of the mixture.

frying
Heat the oil to a moderate heat for deep frying. Fry a few kachoris at a time, turning over until the pastry is crisp. Remove with a slotted spoon on to a paper towel.

Serve with a chutney of your choice.

🏵 Petis This mashed potato snack is a winner with kids

SERVES 6

PREPARATION TIME 20 MINS   COOKING TIME 40 MINS

1lb (450gm) potatoes *(boiled & mashed)*

1/4lb (110gm) frozen peas *(coarsely ground)*

1/4lb (110gm) carrots *(coarsely ground in a processor)*

1 onion *(finely chopped)*

1 tbsp rice flour

1/2 tsp fresh ginger *(crushed)*

1/2 tsp garlic *(crushed)*

2 tbsp gram flour

1 tsp green chillies *(finely crushed)*

1/2 tsp cinnamon powder

2 tbsp lemon juice

1/4 bunch coriander *(finely chopped)*

Oil for deep-frying

1/2 tsp sugar

1/2 tsp salt

method for filling Heat 2 tbsp of oil in a pan.

Add peas, carrots, salt, green chillies, ginger and garlic to the oil. Mix well and let the mixture cook on a low heat for 10 mins, stirring occasionally. Allow to cool.

When cool add sugar, cinnamon powder and lemon juice and mix thoroughly again.

The filling for the petis is now ready. Divide the filling into 12 portions.

method for the potato pastry Add salt, rice flour and gram flour to the mashed potatoes and blend well. Divide the dough into 24 portions.

method for making the petis Take 2 portions of pastry and form two flat round pieces (3in-75mm) with your hands (smear a little oil on your hands when doing this).

Place one portion of the mixture (filling) in the centre of one of the rounds and cover it with the other round pastry piece. Seal the edges with your finger tips.

Mould the pastry into a ball shape by gently rolling it between your palms, in a circular motion.

Continue to do this with the rest of the mixture.

frying Heat the oil to a moderate heat and deep fry the petis, turning on both sides until golden brown. Remove with a slotted spoon onto a paper towel.

Serve with the tamarind and dates chutney.

🦁 Dhokhra A savoury rice cake

Served hot or cold, can be prepared well in advance of the meal.

SERVES 4

PREPARATION TIME 10 MINS   COOKING TIME 45 MINS

½lb (225gm) gram flour
7oz (200gm) plain yogurt
Pinch turmeric powder
1 tsp fresh ginger (crushed)
1½ tsp green chillies (crushed)
2 tsp mustard seeds
4 tsp sesame seeds
5 sprigs fresh coriander (for garnish)

5-6 limdi leaves (optional)
1 tbsp desiccated coconut
1 tsp bicarbonate of soda
½ tsp red chilli powder (for garnish)
5 tbsp oil
1 tsp salt
1 tsp sugar
7 tbsp water

method

Add yogurt, ginger, chillies, salt, turmeric, sugar, and 2 tbsp oil to the gram flour and mix well to form a thick batter. Leave to ferment for 5-6 hours but this is not compulsory.

Take the batter in a bowl, add bicarbonate of soda and whisk thoroughly.

Place the batter in a well-greased baking tray about 12 inch (300mm) diameter or square and 1 inch (25mm) deep. Sprinkle with the red chilli powder and place the tray in a steamer. Line the inside of the lid with a cloth to avoid any moisture dropping in to the batter. Cook for 20 mins on a high heat. Check that the air does not escape.

To check if it is cooked insert a sharp knife into the dhokra, if it comes out clean then the dhokra is cooked.

Remove from heat, let the dhokra cool before turning it out onto a flat surface. Slice the dhokra into 12 squares and transfer the pieces into a large bowl.

Heat the remaining 3 tbsp oil in a pan and add mustard seeds. When popped add sesame seeds and limdi leaves. Remove from heat and pour the sizzled mixture evenly on to the dhokra and mix well but gently to avoid damaging the dhokhras.

garnish

Sprinkle with desiccated coconut and fresh coriander. Serve hot or cold with coconut chutney.

Tip: *The bicarbonate of soda should be added just before the steaming begins.*

✿ Patra   Our most popular starter

Can be served steamed, deep-fried or stir-fried.

SERVES 8
PREPARATION TIME 45 MINS   COOKING TIME 160 MINS (INC STEAMING TIME)

24 large patra leaves
½lb (225gm) gram flour
½lb (225gm) medium wheat flour
3 tsp fresh ginger *(crushed)*
4 tsp chilli powder
2 tsp ajmo *(carom seed)*
7oz (200gm) plain yoghurt
3 tbsp peanuts *(coarsely ground)* optional
3 tsp garlic *(crushed)*
1 tsp turmeric powder
1 tsp cumin and coriander powder
8 tbsp oil
2 tsp fennel seeds
Juice of 2 lemons

1 tsp baking powder
4 tsp sugar
2 tbsp salt
¼ pt (140ml) water

Stir-fried patra:
2 tsp mustard seeds
4 tsp sesame seeds
1 large onion *(finely chopped)*
2 tbsp desiccated coconut *(for garnish)*
5 sprigs coriander *(for garnish)*
Juice of 1 lemon
8 tbsp oil
3 tsp sugar

method

Blend the gram flour and wheat flour with all the ingredients except the patra leaves by adding water to form a thick paste.

Wash the patra leaves under running water. Dry them with a cloth. Remove all the purple or white veins with a sharp knife, making sure not to damage the leaves too much.

Take three patra leaves and place them on the work surface with shiny sides down and pointed end towards you. Spread the paste liberally on one of the leaves, then place a second leaf on top of the pasted leaf and apply more paste as before. Repeat with the third leaf.

Fold the two edges lengthwise towards the middle, to form a rectangular shaped strip. Apply more paste to the folded sides. Take the top end of the rectangular strip and form a tight roll, sealing the pointed end with some paste. Continue to do the same with the rest of the patra leaves.

Steam the patra rolls in a steamer for 2 hrs or in a pressure cooker for ½ hour. Remove from the cooker and let the rolls cool down completely to firm up. Cut them into ½ inch (12mm) thick slices.

deep fried patra Heat the oil for deep frying to a high heat. Fry the patra slices until golden brown on both sides. Remove and place on a paper towel. The crunchy patras can be served with any tangy chutney of your choice.

stir-fried patra Heat the oil in a large pan and add mustard seeds. When popped add sesame seeds and the chopped onions. Stir well.

Chop the sliced patra into four pieces each and add them to the onion mixture. Stir well and let it cook for a further 5 mins. Remove from heat, add the sugar and lemon juice and stir gently to avoid breaking up the cubes.

Garnish with desiccated coconut and coriander before serving with tamarind sauce.

Tips: *Patra leaves are bought in bundles of small or large sized leaves.*

All the leaves must be used up once the wrapping is removed.

Patra can be frozen at the uncooked stage (i.e. before steaming). Place them in the freezer on a tray. Once frozen they can be stored in an appropriate container for future use.

Steam patra straight from frozen.

✿ Makai-no-Chevdo Stir fried sweetcorn with sev

SERVES 4

PREPARATION TIME 10 MINS   COOKING TIME 20 MINS

1lb (450gm) frozen sweetcorn kernels
1 tsp mustard seeds
1 tsp green chillies *(crushed)*
Juice of ½ lemon
2 slices of lemon *(for garnish)*
1 small onion *(finely chopped)*
4 sprigs coriander *(finely chopped)*
¼ lb (110gm) sev *(vermicelli-like savoury made from chickpea flour, available from most Asian shops)*
½ tsp salt
2 tbsp oil

method

Heat the oil in a pan and add mustard seeds. When popped add sweetcorn, salt and green chillies. Stir and let it cook for 15 mins on a low heat.

Remove from the heat, add lemon juice and mix well.

Put sweetcorn mixture onto the serving dish and garnish with sev, onion, fresh coriander and lemon slices on top. Serve hot or cold.

Marcha chillies are *useful* for *indigestion* and joint disorders

Chutneys

Tomato & mint chutney   43

Coconut chutney   43

Tamarind & date chutney   44

Carrot chutney   44

Peanut chutney   45

Coriander & mint chutney   45

*C*hutneys can be made from almost any types of fruits, nuts, vegetables and beans. The taste varies from sweet and sour to hot and spicy. Texture ranges from a thinnish sauce to a thick pulpy texture, depending on what the chutney is made from and the dish with which the chutney is to be served.

Chutney is served with most snacks or eaten with the main meal to provide a sharp contrast in taste.

Some dishes would be incomplete without the chutneys for example Idli, Dahi Vada, Bhel, and Chaat.

Left over chutneys can be frozen for future use.

🏵 Tomato and Mint Chutney

Simple chutney which can be served with most bhajiyas.

SERVES 4
PREPARATION AND MIXING TIME 10 MINS

5 tbsp tomato ketchup
1 small onion *(finely chopped)*
1/2 tsp chilli powder

1 1/2 tsp commercial mint sauce
1/4 pt (140ml) water

method Add all the ingredients in a bowl and mix well so that the ketchup dissolves into the water.

🏵 Coconut Chutney

Ideal with Masala Dhosa.

SERVES 4–6
PREPARATION AND MIXING TIME 20 MINS

1/2 fresh coconut *(shelled & grated)*
or 8oz (225gm) desiccated coconut
3/4 bunch fresh coriander *(chopped)*
5 green chillies *(more if you prefer it hot)*
7oz (200gm) carton plain yoghurt

10 limdi leaves *(optional)*
1/2 tsp sugar
1/2 tsp salt
1/2 pt (280ml) water

method Combine the coconut, green chillies, limdi leaves and coriander in a blender and process until smooth.

Add the yoghurt and continue to blend until the consistency is that of a thick cream. You may need to add a little water to acquire this consistency. Transfer into a bowl, add sugar, salt and mix well.

❧ Tamarind and Date Chutney

A sweet and sour chutney, can be used with most starters.

SERVES 6–8
PREPARATION AND MIXING TIME 10 MINS (INC BOILING TIME)

3oz (85gm) tamarind
4oz (110gm) dates *(deseeded)*
1 tsp cumin and coriander powder
2 tsp chilli powder

6-7 sprigs coriander *(finely chopped)*
1/2 tsp salt
1/2 pt (280ml) water

method

Boil the tamarind in 1/2 pt (280ml) water and dates in 3/4 pt (420ml) water <u>separately</u> for 10 minutes and allow to cool. When cooled mash and squeeze the tamarind until the tamarind is separated from the fibres and forms a thick pulp. Pour into a sieve and again push it through the sieve with your fingers or the bottom of a spoon.

Scrape the bottom of the sieve to collect as much pulp as possible and discard the roughage. Repeat the same process with the dates.

Mix both the pulps together in a bowl, add salt, chilli powder, cumin, coriander powder, fresh coriander and 1/2 pt (280ml) water and mix well.

❧ Carrot Chutney

Can be mixed with fillings for sandwiches and toasties.

SERVES 4
PREPARATION AND MIXING TIME 15 MINS

3 medium sized carrots *(peeled and chopped)*
2 cloves garlic *(chopped)*
1 tsp chilli powder
2 tbsp tomato ketchup

Juice of 1/2 lemon
1/2 tsp sugar
1/2 pt (280ml) water
1/2 tsp salt

method

Process the carrots and garlic in a food processor, adding water to form a thick smooth sauce. Pour into a bowl and add sugar, salt, chilli powder, lemon juice and tomato ketchup and mix well.

 Peanut Chutney

A good alternative to tomato and mint chutney.

SERVES 6

PREPARATION AND MIXING TIME 15 MINS

8oz (225gm) peanuts
3/4 bunch fresh coriander *(chopped)*
2 cloves garlic *(chopped)*
6-7 green chillies

Juice of 1/2 lemon
1 tsp of sugar
1 tsp of salt
1/2 pt (280ml) water

method Place the peanuts in a food processor and chop finely. Add fresh coriander, garlic, chillies and continue to process by adding a little water to get the consistency of double cream. Transfer into a bowl and add sugar, salt and lemon and mix well.

Coriander and Mint Chutney

A spicy chutney to spice up your sandwich or toastie fillings.

SERVES 6

PREPARATION AND MIXING TIME 15 MINS

1 bunch fresh coriander
1/2 bunch fresh mint *(or 2 tsp of commercial mint sauce)*
5 green chillies
1 tsp sugar
1/2 tsp salt
1/2 pt (280ml) water

method Combine all the ingredients in a food processor and process. Add water to get the consistency of double cream. Transfer into a bowl and mix well.

Garlic - lassun
is good for
joint pains
and *coughs*

Specialities

Pani Puri   48

Channa Bateta   50

Dahi Vada   51

Masala Dhosa   52

Ondhwo   54

These specialities are larger than the starters and form a very filling snack for your elevenses or when you don't fancy cooking a whole meal.

They also provide a pleasant change from the usual fritters or other fried starters.

Dahi Vada in particular forms a perfect accompaniment to most main course curries. In the south of India, the Masala Dhosa is very popular and is eaten for breakfast, lunch or evening meal.

🌹 Pani Puri Meaning water puri

A wholesome snack, unique to Gujarat.

SERVES 6–8

PREPARATION TIME 30 MINS   COOKING TIME 110 MINS

Puri dough:
¼ lb (110gm) plain flour
2oz (55gm) semolina *(fine)*
Oil for deep frying
½ tsp salt
15 tbsp water

Stuffing:
¼ lb (110gm) boiled red
chickpeas
2 medium potatoes *(boiled &
chopped into very small cubes)*
1 medium onion *(finely chopped)*
1½ tsp chilli powder
3 tbsp sugar
1½ tsp salt

Tamarind sauce:
3oz (75gm) dried tamarind
1½ tbsp sugar
½ tsp chilli powder
½ tsp cumin & coriander powder
½ pt (280ml) water

method for puri dough Mix the flour, semolina and salt in a bowl.

Make the dough with cold water. The dough should be kneaded until soft (similar to pastry dough) and left for half an hour for it to rest.

Divide the dough into five portions. On a well greased surface, roll one of the portions into a big, thin circle (15 inch - 400mm diameter). Cut as many 2 inch (50mm) diameter circles as you can, using an appropriate cutter.

frying

Heat the oil and leave on a high heat until the oil is ready. Slide the puris into the oil one at a time. Turn down heat to a low setting to avoid the puris burning.

Pat the puris with the bottom of a slotted spoon to encourage them to puff up. (Not all the puris will puff up). Continue to fry, turning a few times, until both sides are golden brown. Remove from oil and place on a paper towel to soak up the excess oil. Continue until all the dough is used up.

method for stuffing   Mix the potatoes, onions and chick peas in a bowl. Add chilli powder, salt, sugar and mix well. The stuffing is now ready .

method for tamarind sauce   Boil the tamarind in a pan until soft. Take it off the heat and allow to cool down. When cool, squash the fibres with your fingers to separate the pulp and push it through a sieve over a bowl. A thick pulp should collect in the bowl.

Add the water, chilli powder and sugar to the pulp and mix well.

The tamarind sauce is now ready .

how to eat the Pani Puris   Break open the upper crust of the puffed puri from the centre to create a hole. Stuff with chick pea mixture and 1 tsp of the tamarind sauce.

Place the whole puri into the mouth to experience the crunchy sweet and sour taste.

NB: In India people prefer to dunk the whole puri, with the mixture inside, into a bowl of the tamarind sauce and then put the whole puri in the mouth all at once. The sauce is thinned down to a watery (pani – meaning water) consistency.

❧ Channa Bateta

A very popular snack with most Gujaratis.

SERVES 4

PREPARATION TIME 30 MINS   COOKING TIME 25 MINS

½ lb (225gm) kabuli channa *(white chick peas)*
or ½ lb (225gm) tinned chickpeas *(washed)*
1 tbsp gram flour
1 tsp green chillies *(crushed)*
1 pkt (200gm) creamed coconut *(grated)*
Juice of ½ lemon
½ tbsp tomato puree
1 medium potato *(par-boiled, peeled and chopped into small cubes)*

2 tbsp oil
1 tsp salt
1 pt (560ml) water

Garnish:
2 small onions *(finely chopped)*
¼ lb (110gm) fried peanuts
3 pkts (75gm) potato crisps *(crushed)*

method

Soak the chickpeas overnight in hot water, bring to the boil and cook until soft, then drain. If tinned chickpeas are used just wash them in cold running water.

Heat the oil in a pan then turn down the heat.

Add the gram flour and fry until slightly brown.

Add the tomato puree, green chillies, salt and water and bring to the boil.

Add the chickpeas and potatoes and mix well.

Add creamed coconut and lemon juice. Stir well and cover the pan.

Cook for 20 minutes or until the potatoes are tender.

The channa bateta mix is now ready.

Before serving, garnish with potato crisps, onions and peanuts to taste.

🌸 Dahi Vada

Yoghurt dumplings are a perfect accompaniment to most curries or they can be eaten as a snack.

SERVES 6
PREPARATION TIME 85 MINS (INC SOAKING TIME)   COOKING TIME 40 MINS

Vada mix:
1/2 lb (225gm) chora daal *(split black-eyed beans)*
1/4 lb (110gm) maag daal *(shelled)*
1 tsp green chillies *(crushed)*
1 1/2 tsp salt
Oil for deep frying

Yoghurt sauce:
2 15oz (425gm) cartons plain yoghurt
2 tsp mustard seeds
2 tsp cumin seeds
1/2 tbsp chilli powder *(for garnish)*
3-4 sprigs coriander *(finely chopped for garnish)*
2 tbsp oil
5 tbsp sugar
1/4 pt (140ml) water
1/2 tsp salt

method for vadas
Soak chora daal and maag daal separately, for 1 hour.

Drain and grind the chora daal and the maag daal in small quantities at a time, adding 2 tbsp of water during the grinding. Repeat the process until both the daals are finished. The mixture should be like a paste by now. Add the green chillies and salt and mix well.

Divide the mixture into 14 portions. Heat the oil for deep frying to a moderate heat. Take a portion of the mixture in your palm and form a ball and slide it into the oil. Deep-fry a few at a time, turning them until they are golden brown all over. Remove from the frying pan and place onto a paper towel to soak up the excess oil. They are now known as vadas.

Soak all the vadas in a bowl of hot water for 10-15 mins. The vadas will now puff up.

Remove the vadas from the water, one at a time, and gently squeeze the excess water out on a paper towel and place them in a large serving dish. The vadas are now ready for dressing with the yoghurt sauce.

method for yoghurt sauce
Put the yoghurt in a large bowl.

Heat the oil in a pan. Add the mustard seeds to the oil, cover the pan and wait until the seeds have popped. Add the cumin seeds to the pan and remove from the heat. Pour this hot oil and the sugar on to the yoghurt and mix well. Pour the yoghurt sauce garnish on to the vadas in the serving dish.

Garnish with the chilli powder and the fresh coriander and serve.

🏵 Masala Dhosa

This South Indian pancake is a meal in itself. I have adapted it to my taste.

SERVES 8

MASALA PREPARATION TIME 10 MINS   COOKING TIME 40 MINS
SAMBHAR PREPARATION TIME 25 MINS   COOKING TIME 40 MINS
DHOSA PREPARATION TIME 10 MINS   COOKING TIME 30 MINS

Pancake:
4oz (110gm) rice flour *(fine)*
4oz (110gm) urad flour *(fine)*
$1/4$ tsp salt
$1^{1}/4$ pt (700ml) water

Mixed Vegetable Stuffing:
$1/2$ lb (225gm) mixed veg *(frozen, boiled and drained)*
3 medium potatoes *(boiled, peeled and diced)*
2 medium onions *(finely chopped)*
1 tsp chilli powder
juice of 1 lemon
2 tsp cumin seeds
1 tsp sugar
6 tbsp oil
$1^{1}/2$ tsp salt

Sambhar:
$1/2$ lb (225gm) mixed vegetables *(frozen)*
$1/2$ lb (225gm) tuwer daal *(split Pigeon peas)*
2 tsp ginger *(crushed)*
2 tsp green chillies *(ground)*
$1/2$ tsp turmeric powder *(hardar)*
$1/2$ tsp hing (asafoetida) powder
4-5 dried red chillies
3-4 cloves
14oz (400gm) tin tomatoes *(liquidised)*
1 tsp mustard seeds
juice of 2 lemons
2 tsp sugar
3 tbsp oil
1 tsp salt

Garnish:
4 large carrots *(grated)*
4 tbsp desiccated coconut

method for dhosa (pancake)
Mix the rice flour and the urad flour in a bowl. Add water and whisk the mixture to a smooth batter with the consistency of single cream.

Heat a griddle or a heavy frying pan to a moderate heat. Dab a clean cloth or paper towel in oil and grease the surface of the griddle.

Pour the batter with a $1/4$ pt (140ml) ladle into the centre of the griddle and quickly spread it into a thin layer. Cover the dhosa with a lid until it starts to come away from the surface of the griddle. Dribble a tsp of oil around the edge to avoid the pancake sticking to the griddle.

Turn over the dhosa and cook until golden brown and slightly crispy. Put 2 tbsp (or more if you like) of the stuffing (see below) in the centre of the dhosa, sprinkle with 2 tbsp of chopped onions and roll the dhosa into an open-ended pancake. Allow to cook for a further 2-3 minutes until the stuffing is hot as well.

Remove to a serving dish by gently sliding it off the griddle. Garnish with carrots and desiccated coconut before serving, with coconut chutney and sambhar (see below).

method for masala (stuffing)
Heat the oil in a pan. Add the cumin seeds and let them sizzle until golden brown. Add the mixed veg and potatoes to the pan and mix well. Add the rest of the ingredients except for the onions and mix again.

Cover the pan and allow to cook for 5-10 mins at a low heat, stirring occasionally. Put to one side until the dhosa is ready.

method for sambhar
Soak the tuwer daal for 20 mins, wash and boil until tender. Liquidise the boiled daal. Add ginger, green chillies, salt, turmeric, sugar and mixed veg to the daal and bring to the boil.

In a separate pan, heat the oil and add the mustard seeds and allow them to pop. Add dried red chillies, cloves and hing and stir well. Add the mixture to the daal and simmer for 10-15 mins. Add the lemon juice.

Tip: *The masala and the sambhar can be prepared the day before.*

❀ Ondhwo

This Gujarati savoury cake makes a superb starter eaten hot or cold.

SERVES 4-6

PREPARATION TIME 30 MINS   COOKING TIME 80 MINS

8oz (225gm) ondhwo flour
1/4lb (110gm) sweetcorn kernels *(coarsely crushed)*
2 carrots *(grated)*
2 small potatoes *(finely chopped)*
2 small onions *(finely chopped)*
15oz (425gm) plain yoghurt
2 tsp ginger *(crushed)*
3 tsp green chillies *(crushed)*
1 bunch fresh coriander *(finely chopped)*
2 tsp bicarbonate of soda

1/4 tsp turmeric
2 tsp mustard seeds
2 tsp cumin seeds
6 tbsp sesame seeds
1 tbsp desiccated coconut *(for garnish)*
1 tsp sugar
8 tbsp oil
2 tsp salt
3/8 pt (200ml) warm water

method

Combine the ondhwo flour, yoghurt and water in a bowl.

Add salt, sugar, turmeric and green chillies. Mix well and leave to ferment for 12 hours or overnight.

Add all the vegetables to the fermented mixture.

Add the bicarbonate of soda and mix well again.

Transfer the mixture into a greased baking tray about 12 inch (300mm) diameter or square and 1 inch deep and set aside. This can now be called Ondhwo.

Heat the 8 tbsp of oil in a small pan adding the mustard seeds. When the mustard seeds have popped add the cumin seeds and coriander and stir well. Keep stirring until the coriander turns a dark green colour. Now spread this mixture evenly over the Ondhwo mix in the baking tray.

Sprinkle the sesame seeds evenly over the mixture and bake in a pre-heated oven for 30 mins at gas mark 6 (200°C/400°F).

To check if the Ondhwo is cooked insert a sharp knife into it. If the blade comes out clean, the dish is ready.

Remove the Ondhwo from the oven and let it cool for 30 minutes. Cut into squares and garnish with coriander and desiccated coconut before serving with a chutney of your choice.

Aubergine - ringans
are *useful* in combating *fever*
and easing *digestion* during
loss of appetite

Shak - Main Course Vegetable Curries

Ful Cobi - cauliflower   58

Posho - Greenbeans, sweetcorn & carrot curry   59

Bhaji - spinach   60

Cobi Mattar - cabbage, potato & peas   61

Ravaiya - stuffed aubergines   63

Bateta - dry potato curry   64

Ringan Mattar - aubergine & pea curry   65

Ondhiyu - traditional Gujarati mixed vegetables   67

*V*egetables in the UK have become very exotic over the last decade, with fresh vegetables imported from all corners of the world overnight. Some of the Indian Greengrocers, especially in London, are open 24 hours a day to provide the freshest vegetables at all times of the day, from countries as far apart as China, India, Kenya and the West Indies (to name but a few). Each vegetable has its own unique taste and can be turned into a delicious curry, using the correct aromatic spices to enhance their flavours.

Fresh vegetables, properly cooked, are the basis of good eating anywhere in the world, bursting with energy-giving vitamins, minerals and carbohydrates. Vegetables start losing their nutrients from the moment they are picked, so they must be cooked and eaten as soon as practically possible. Sturdy tubers such as beets, carrots, yams, potatoes, etc. could be stored in a paper bag and kept in a cool dark store. Greens are best stored in sealed plastic bags, in a fridge.

Purists would recommend that the dishes cooked should be served immediately, avoiding re-heating whenever possible, since re-heating breaks down the fibres and increases the loss of nutrients. If dishes are to be cooked in advance then allow them to cool down to room temperature and seal them in an air-tight container and refrigerate immediately. To minimise the changes, re-heat in a steamer or a double boiler if you have one.

🌸 Ful Cobi Cauliflower, carrot & pea curry

SERVES 4

PREPARATION TIME 30 MINS   COOKING TIME 25 MINS

1 medium sized cauliflower *(trimmed and
cut into florets)*

2 small potatoes *(cubed)*

4oz (110gm) frozen peas *(defrosted and drained)*

1 carrot *(peeled and cubed)*

1½ tsp ginger *(crushed)*

1 tsp garlic *(crushed)*

1 tsp green chillies *(crushed)*

½ tsp turmeric powder

1 tsp cumin and coriander powder

2-3 sprigs coriander *(finely chopped for garnish)*

1 tsp mustard seeds

7 tbsp oil

1¼ tsp salt

method

Heat the oil in a pan, add mustard seeds and fry until mustard seeds pop.

Add all the vegetables and spices except coriander. Mix well, lower the heat and cover the pan.

Cook for 20-25 minutes or until vegetables are tender.

Before serving garnish with coriander.

Since this is a dry curry serve with chappatis or puris.

Tip: *The Daal sauce (p89) is often served with this curry.*

❀ Posho Greenbeans, sweetcorn and carrot curry

SERVES 4

PREPARATION TIME 15 MINS   COOKING TIME 25 MINS

1lb (450gm) sliced green beans *(fresh or frozen)*

8oz (250gm) sweetcorn kernels

2 carrots *(cut into tiny cubes or julienned)*

1 tsp carom seeds *(ajmo)*

1½ tsp ginger *(crushed)*

1 tsp garlic *(crushed)*

½ tsp turmeric powder

1 tsp cumin and coriander powder

2 tsp green chillies *(crushed)*

2-3 sprigs coriander *(finely chopped for garnish)*

6 tbsp oil

1 tsp salt

method Heat the oil in a pan. Add carom seeds. When brown, add green beans, sweetcorn, carrots and all the spices. Mix well.

Lower the heat, cover the pan and cook for 25-30 minutes or until the vegetables are tender, stirring occasionally.

Garnish with fresh coriander before serving.

Tip: *Leftovers of this dish make great toasties.*

🌸 Bhaji Spinach

SERVES 4-5

PREPARATION TIME 30 MINS   COOKING TIME 30 MINS

1lb (450gm) frozen spinach

2 medium sized onions *(finely chopped)*

2 tbsp tomato puree *(diluted in 1/4 pt (140ml) water)*

1 potato *(peeled and cubed)*

2 tsp ginger *(crushed)*

2 tsp garlic *(crushed)*

1/2 tsp chilli powder

2 tsp cumin and coriander powder

3 sprigs coriander *(finely chopped for garnish)*

1 1/2 tsp turmeric powder

1 1/2 tsp garam masala

1 tsp of dried fenugreek seeds

4 tbsp of oil

1 1/2 tsp salt

method

Heat the oil in a pan. Add fenugreek seeds. As they turn brown, add onions and fry until the onions turn soft but not brown.

Add the tomato puree and the rest of the spices and mix well.

Let the sauce simmer for 5-6 minutes, add the spinach and potatoes and mix well into the sauce.

Cover the pan, lower the heat and cook for 20-25 minutes, stirring frequently.

Serve with coriander garnishing.

Tip: *Kadhi sauce (p89) is usually served with this curry. Khichadi rice (p85) makes a perfect accompaniment.*

Spinach - bhaji

contains a

rich source of *iron*

🦁 Cobi Mattar Cabbage, Potatoes and Peas

SERVES 4-5

PREPARATION TIME 20 MINS   COOKING TIME 20 MINS

2lb (900gm) hard cabbage *(shredded)*
1lb (450gm) frozen peas *(washed and drained)*
1 medium potato *(peeled and diced)*
2 tsp ginger *(crushed)*
1 tsp garlic *(crushed)*
2 tsp green chillies *(crushed)*

$1/2$ tsp turmeric powder
3 sprigs fresh coriander *(finely chopped for garnish)*
1 tsp cumin and coriander powder
$1^1/_2$ tsp of mustard seeds
8 tbsp of cooking oil
2 tsp salt

method

Heat the oil in a pan, add the mustard seeds. When the mustard seeds pop and turn grey, lower the heat and add the cabbage, potato and peas.

Add all the spices, except for the fresh coriander, and mix well.

Cover the pan and cook for 20-25 mins on a low heat, stirring frequently until the potatoes are tender.

Garnish with fresh coriander before serving.

🏵 Ravaiya A mouthwatering stuffed aubergine curry

Kenyan aubergines are ideal for this dish because they are more succulent and will soak up the spices from the stuffing more readily than other varieties of aubergines.

SERVES 4

PREPARATION TIME 60 MINS   COOKING TIME 50 MINS

6 Kenyan aubergines *(normally round in shape)*
2 medium potatoes *(finely chopped)*
2 medium onions *(finely chopped)*
2 handfuls peanuts *(crushed)*
2 tsp ginger *(crushed)*
2 tsp garlic *(crushed)*
1 tsp chilli powder
1 tsp turmeric powder
1 tsp cumin and coriander powder

1 tsp garam masala
2 tsp tomato puree
or 1 14oz (400gm) tin tomatoes *(liquidised)*
3 sticks cinnamon
1/4 bunch fresh coriander *(finely chopped)*
2 fresh tomatoes cut into wedges *(for garnish)*
12 tbsp oil
1 1/2 tsp salt

method for stuffing
Transfer the potatoes, onions, peanuts, ginger, garlic, chilli powder, salt, turmeric, cumin, coriander powder, garam masala, half the fresh coriander and 2 tbsp oil into a bowl. Mix well. (If using your hands make sure to wear some disposable gloves as the turmeric and the chilli will stain your hands for a long time.)

Gently remove the leaves from the bottom of the aubergine stem and scrape the stem slightly, but do not remove the stem completely. Make a cross slit three quarters of the length down the aubergine without separating at the stem end.

Fill the aubergines with the stuffing, gently pressing it down the slit, making sure the aubergines don't break. Leave the remaining stuffing aside.

method for cooking
Use a pan which is large enough to arrange the aubergines in a single layer. Heat the remaining oil in a pan and add the cinnamon sticks. As soon as the cinnamon changes colour, add the stuffing and the tomatoes and mix well. Turn the heat down to very low.

Arrange the stuffed aubergines on top of the stuffing in a single layer and cover the pan. Cook the aubergines for 50 mins, occasionally turning them so they are cooked evenly on all sides.

Remove the cooked aubergines on the side. Transfer the stuffing from the pan on to a serving dish. Arrange the aubergines on top of the stuffing, garnish with tomato wedges and coriander. Serve with rotli or khichadi and kadhi.

Bateta Dry Potato Curry

SERVES 4

PREPARATION TIME 10 MINS   COOKING TIME 10 MINS

2 large potatoes *(peeled and cut into cubes or chip shaped)*
1½ tsp ginger *(crushed)*
1 tsp garlic *(crushed)*
1 tsp turmeric powder
½ tsp coriander and cumin powder
1¼ tsp of cumin seeds
1 tsp green chillies *(crushed)*
3 sprigs fresh coriander *(finely chopped-for garnish)*
10 tbsp of cooking oil
1¼ tsp salt

method

Heat the oil in a shallow pan (preferably a frying pan).

Add the cumin seeds and let them sizzle and when the colour changes to brown add the coriander and cumin powder and stir-fry for ½ minute.

Lower the heat and add the rest of the spices and the potatoes, and mix well.

Cover the pan and let it cook on a low heat for 10 minutes or until the potatoes become tender, frequently stirring gently with a flat spoon.

Garnish with coriander before serving.

Tip: *This curry makes a perfect filling for toasties. Bateta curry tastes divine mixed with plain rice and daal sauce (p79).*

🌸 Ringan Mattar Aubergine and Pea Curry

SERVES 4

PREPARATION TIME 20 MINS   COOKING TIME 25 MINS

1 large aubergine *(cut into chunky pieces)*
3/4lb (330gm) frozen peas
1 tsp ginger *(crushed)*
1 tsp garlic *(crushed)*
1 tsp mustard seeds
1 tsp turmeric powder
1 tsp cumin and coriander powder
1 tsp red chillies
1 8oz (225gm) tin tomatoes *(liquidised)*
5 tbsp cooking oil
1 1/2 tsp salt
1/4pt (140ml) water
3 sprigs fresh coriander *(finely chopped for garnish)*

method
Heat the oil in a pan and add the mustard seeds. When the mustard seeds pop and turn grey, add the tomatoes and the rest of the spices.

Let the mixture simmer for 5-6 minutes or until the oil starts to separate from the mixture.

Add the aubergine chunks and peas and mix well.

Cover the pan and let it cook for 20-25 minutes on a low heat, stirring frequently.

Serve with a coriander garnish.

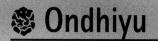# Ondhiyu

A traditional Gujarati mixed vegetable dish.

SERVES 4

PREPARATION TIME 60 MINS   COOKING TIME 40 MINS

¹/₄ lb (110gm) guwar *(remove ends and break into half)*

¹/₄ lb (110gm) valor *(remove ends and open pods)*

¹/₄ lb (110gm) papadi *(remove ends and open pods)*

¹/₄ lb (110gm) giloda *(thinly sliced)*

1 medium potato *(quartered)*

1 medium sweet potato *(quartered)*

6 baby aubergines *(make a slit in the middle)*

1 corn on the cob *(fresh or frozen, but must be pre-boiled and cut into small pieces)*

1 tsp ajmo *(carom seeds)*

2 tbsp sesame seeds

1¹/₂ tsp ginger *(crushed)*

1 handful peanuts *(optional)*

1¹/₂ tsp garlic *(crushed)*

1 tsp turmeric powder

1¹/₂ tsp green chillies *(crushed)*

1¹/₂ tsp cumin and coriander powder

1 14oz (400gm) tin tomatoes *(liquidised)*

8-10 tbsp oil

1¹/₂ tsp salt

For koftas:

¹/₂ bunch fresh fenugreek *(finely chopped)*

¹/₄ tsp chilli powder

4 tbsp gram flour

¹/₂ tbsp oil

Oil for deep-frying

¹/₄ tsp salt

2-3 tbsp water

Tip: *Guwar, valor, giloda and papadi will only be available in specialist shops. They could be replaced by the same weight of a mixture of any of the following: broad beans, french beans, runner beans, mange tout peas and courgettes.*

method for koftas
Take a large bowl and add all the ingredients (except the water) and ¹/₂ tbsp oil to the fenugreek. Mix well with the fingertips.

Add water to form a sticky paste. Wash your hands. Make the mixture into small balls. Continue to do this until all the mixture is used up.

Deep fry the balls for 2-3 minutes. Remove with a slotted spoon and lay them on a paper towel. The koftas are ready.

method for the curry
Heat the oil in a pan, add the ajmo and sesame seeds. (Cover the pan as the sesame seeds will splutter). When the seeds have sizzled and changed colour, remove from the heat.

Add all the vegetables, peanuts and spices and mix well. Cover the pan and cook for 20 mins or until the vegetables are tender. Add the koftas and cook for a further 10 mins.

Garnish with chopped coriander before serving.

Beans are rich in *proteins,* minerals and *vitamin B*

Kathor - Beans and Daals

Chora and mushroom   71

Vaal   72

Dry channa daal   73

Bhagat muthiya   75

Maag daal   76

Garam masala daal   77

*K*athor simply means beans and split beans. India produces the largest selection of pulses in the world. Once the bean is split it is called a daal, so when a mung bean is split it is called mung daal. Beans are wholesome when cooked whereas daal dishes are more like a thick broth. Daals are either shelled or unshelled. Beans and pulses are eaten as a main meal. Most beans can be sprouted and used for creating a new variety of dishes or can be used in salads e.g. mung bean sprouts.

Some of the chutneys and savoury snacks have been created from beans and daals.

Most beans can be turned into flour to create an even bigger variety of ingredients, the most common being gram flour made from chickpeas, which is used for making the batter for all the bhajiyas (fritters).

Most whole beans would need to be soaked in warm water before cooking. Soaking time depends upon the type of bean: eg, kidney beans, vaal beans, soya beans and chickpeas all need soaking for more than twelve hours before cooking.

Daals can be cooked without soaking most of the time, but if used for cooking dry daal curries, it is advisable to soak for at least $1/2$ an hour in warm water beforehand. Beans and daals both cook more quickly in a pressure cooker (nearly half the time).

Nowadays, most beans and some daals are available in tins, already boiled and soaked in brine to act as a preservative. When using tinned beans make sure that all the excess salt from the brine is washed off before cooking.

❦ Chora and Mushroom

Black-eyed bean and mushroom curry.

SERVES 4

PREPARATION TIME 60 MINS (INC SOAKING)   COOKING TIME 50 MINS

12oz (340gm) chora *(dried blackeyed beans)*
1½ tbsp gram flour
7 medium mushrooms *(sliced)*
1 tbsp tomato puree
1½ tsp ajmo *(carom seeds)*
1 tsp garlic *(crushed)*
1½ tsp ginger *(crushed)*
1 tsp turmeric

1 tsp cumin and coriander powder
1 tsp chilli powder *(or green chillies)*
1 tsp garam masala *(to garnish)*
3-4 sprigs fresh coriander *(finely chopped for garnish)*
3 tbsp oil
1¼ tsp salt
¾ pt (425ml) water

method

Soak the beans for 1 hour, then boil them until they are tender. Drain and set aside.

Heat the oil in a pan, add the ajmo until it sizzles and turns golden brown.

Add gram flour, stir, then add tomato puree and all the spices.

Simmer for 10 mins, stirring occasionally, then add beans, mushrooms and water. Mix well, bring to the boil, then lower heat and simmer for another 10 mins.

Garnish with garam masala and coriander before serving.

Add extra water if you require more sauce.

🌸 Vaal Curry Haricot bean curry

SERVES 6

PREPARATION TIME 30 MINS (INC BOILING)   COOKING TIME 30 MINS

1lb (450gm) vaal beans
1 14oz (400gm) tin tomatoes *(liquidised)*
1 tbsp gram flour
1 tsp ajmo *(carom seed)*
½ tsp hing *(asafoetida)*
1½ tsp ginger *(crushed)*
1½ tsp garlic *(crushed)*
1 tsp chilli powder

1 tsp cumin and coriander powder
1 tsp turmeric powder
1½ tsp garam masala *(for garnish)*
3-4 sprigs fresh coriander *(finely chopped for garnish)*
3 tbsp oil
1¼ tsp salt
½ pt (280ml) water

method

Soak the vaal beans overnight and boil in 4 pts (2.5l) of water.

Heat the oil in a pan, lower the heat and remove the pan from the heat.

Add ajmo and let it sizzle until it becomes a brownish colour, add hing and gram flour and continue to stir.

Return to the heat and add the tomatoes and the rest of the spices, mixing well.

Let it simmer for 5 mins, add vaal beans and mix well.

Cover the pan and let it boil for 20 mins stirring occasionally.

Transfer into a serving bowl and garnish with garam masala and the coriander.

🏵 Dry Channa Daal Split chickpea curry

SERVES 4

PREPARATION TIME 60 MINS   COOKING TIME 45 MINS

1lb (450gm) channa daal
1 medium onion *(thinly sliced)*
1 tsp mustard seeds
1½ tsp ginger *(crushed)*
1 tsp garlic *(crushed)*
1½ tsp green chilli *(crushed)*
1 tsp turmeric

½ tsp garam masala *(for garnish)*
1 tsp cumin and coriander powder
2-3 sprigs fresh coriander *(finely chopped for garnish)*
10 tbsp oil
1¼ tsp salt
¼ pt (140ml) water

method

Soak the daal in hot water for an hour. Wash and drain.

Heat oil in a pan and add mustard seeds. When they have popped add the channa daal.

Add all the spices and onions, mix well and add water.

Lower the heat, cover the pan and cook for 25-30 mins or until the daal is tender.

Garnish with coriander before serving.

Tip: *Channa daal can also be used as a filling for toasties.*

Once the *bean* is split it is called a *daal*

🪷 Bhagat Muthiya Chickpea koftas with potatoes

SERVES 4

PREPARATION TIME 95 MINS (INC SOAKING)   COOKING TIME 90 MINS

$1/2$lb (225gm) channa daal

1 tbsp gram flour

$1/2$ tsp ginger (crushed)

$1/2$ tsp garlic (crushed)

$1/2$ tsp green chillies (crushed)

$1/2$ tsp cumin and coriander powder

6-7 sprigs fenugreek (finely chopped)

3 tbsp oil

Oil for deep frying

1 tsp salt

Sauce:

1 large onion (chopped)

1 small tomato (diced)

1 tbsp tomato puree

$1 1/4$ tsp chilli powder

1 tsp turmeric powder

1lb (450gm) potatoes (cubed and par-boiled)

$1 1/2$ tsp ginger (crushed)

1 tsp garlic (crushed)

1 tsp cumin and coriander powder

3-4 sprigs fresh coriander (for garnish)

$1 1/2$ tsp garam masala (for garnish)

5 tbsp oil

$1 1/4$ tsp salt

$1 1/4$ pt (700ml) water

method for koftas
Soak the channa daal for 1 hour in hot water, drain and grind the daal in a food processor. Transfer the daal into a bowl and mix with gram flour, all the spices and 3 tbsp oil.

Form the mixture into 16 balls, place on a tray and then deep fry them on medium heat for 4-5 mins.

Remove with a slotted spoon and leave them aside.

method for sauce
Heat the oil in a pan and fry the onion until golden brown, then add the tomatoes and the rest of the spices. Let it simmer for 5-8 mins stirring occasionally.

Add water, mix well and add the koftas and potatoes. Cover the pan and let it simmer for 20 mins stirring occasionally.

Transfer into a serving dish and garnish with garam masala and fresh coriander.

Tip: *Wet the hands when making the balls*

🌹 Maag Daal Split mung bean curry cooked with fenugreek

SERVES 8

PREPARATION TIME 90 MINS (INC SOAKING)   COOKING TIME 45 MINS

1lb (450gm) maag daal *(shelled)*

1 14oz (400gm) tin tomatoes *(liquidised)*

1½ tsp garlic *(crushed)*

1½ tsp ginger *(crushed)*

1 tsp cumin and coriander powder

1 tsp turmeric

1 medium onion *(finely chopped)*

1 bunch fresh fenugreek *(finely chopped)*

1 tsp garam masala *(for garnish)*

3-4 sprigs coriander *(finely chopped for garnish)*

1½ tsp chilli powder

10 tbsp oil

1 tsp salt

2³/₄ pt (1.5l) water

method

Carefully remove any foreign bodies from the daal, soak for 1 hour and boil in 2½ pt of water until tender.

Heat the oil in a pan and fry the onion until golden brown. Add the fenugreek and cook for a further 3 mins.

Add tomatoes and all the spices and mix well. Let it cook for 10-15 mins, stirring occasionally, until a thick sauce forms.

Add the Maag daal and ¼ pt (140ml) water to the sauce, mix well then let it simmer for 10-15 mins.

Garnish with garam masala and fresh coriander before serving.

Turmeric powder -
hardar is

an *antiseptic*

🌸 Garam Masala Daal

Tuwer daal cooked in spicy garam masala.

SERVES 6

PREPARATION TIME 60 MINS (INC SOAKING)   COOKING TIME 60 MINS

½lb (225gm) tuwer daal

1 large onion *(finely chopped)*

1½ tbsp tomato puree *(diluted in ¼ pt (140ml) water)*

1 large potato *(boiled, peeled & finely cubed)*

1½ tsp ginger *(crushed)*

1½ tsp garlic *(crushed)*

1 tsp chilli powder

4 tsp garam masala *(for garnish)*

½ tsp turmeric powder

1 tsp cumin and coriander powder

3 sticks cinnamon

2-3 sprigs of coriander *(finely chopped for garnish)*

8 tbsp oil

3 tsp salt

2¼ pt (1.2l) water

method

Soak the daal for half an hour and wash thoroughly, removing any foreign bodies. Cook for 1 hour (or 15 mins in a pressure cooker), until the daal is tender, using 2pts (1.1l) water.

When cooked use a whisk to give a smooth texture and set it aside.

Heat the oil in a pan. Add the cinnamon sticks and fry until brown.

Add onions and fry, stirring frequently, until golden brown.

Add tomato puree, salt, turmeric, ginger, garlic, chilli powder, cumin and coriander powder. Mix well. Let it simmer on a low heat for 5 minutes.

Add the daal and potatoes and ¼pt (140ml) water and mix well.

Let the daal simmer for 10 mins stirring occasionally.

Garnish with garam masala and fresh coriander and stir before serving.

Serve with batura and coriander rice.

*B*haat or rice is the staple diet for most of the South and West of India. In Gujarat, chappatis are eaten first with the curries followed by rice. Rice is too dry and bland to eat on its own therefore a sauce, usually Daal or Kadhi always accompanies it. If a wet curry is made then rice is mixed with the curry sauce instead to give it some flavour.

There are about 10,000 varieties of rice worldwide, but I have used long-grain Basmati as it is easier to cook, has a soft texture and when cooked it appears fluffy and the grains stay well separated.

Brown rice is healthier since the husk, which contains all the nutrients, has not been removed, but it is difficult to keep it from sticking together during the cooking process so its appearance is not very appetising.

Before cooking remove any foreign bodies from the rice.

As rice has a lot of starch, it needs to be removed. Wash the rice with cold water several times or until the water runs clear.

When boiling the rice add a few drops of oil to help the grains remain separated.

Rice recipes are endless. Once you succeed in cooking plain boiled rice you will be amazed at what can be created with a little imagination. By adding beans, daal, spices and vegetables, rice can be transformed into a very tasty snack or a whole meal in itself.

Medicinal properties: not suitable for people suffering from muscle pains. Rice is believed to slow down the ageing process.

Bhaat - Rice

Plain Boiled Rice   80

Pilau Rice   81

Vegetable Biriyani   83

Coriander Rice   85

Stir-Fried Rice   86

Spinach and Sweetcorn Rice   87

Khichadi   89

Maragi Rice   91

Sauces to go with Rice

Kadhi   92

Daal   93

🌼 Plain Boiled Rice

SERVES 4

PREPARATION TIME 10 MINS   COOKING TIME 15 MINS

12oz (340gm) basmati rice
2-3 sprigs coriander *(finely chopped for garnish)*
2 tsp of oil *(will help keep the grains separate)*
1 tsp salt
4½pts (2.6l) water

method

Wash the rice thoroughly until the water runs clear.

Bring the water to the boil, add rice, salt and oil.

Let the rice cook on a medium heat until it is no longer brittle. Check from time to time that there is plenty of water.

Drain the rice and cover for 2-3 mins. Then transfer into a serving dish by using a flat spoon taking care not to damage the cooked rice.

Traditionally a spoonful of butter or ghee is mixed in the rice before serving to give it a beautiful aroma and keep the rice grains separate.

Gujaratis
love to eat rice
with *daal sauce*

🌸 Pilau Rice

SERVES 4

PREPARATION TIME 15 MINS   COOKING TIME 20 MINS

12oz (340gm) basmati rice
4oz (110gm) mixed vegetables *(e.g. peas, carrots, sweetcorn etc.)*
2 tsp cumin seeds
3 cinnamon sticks
1/4 tsp turmeric
2-3 sprigs fresh coriander *(finely chopped for garnish)*
2 tbsp oil
1 tsp salt
1pt (560ml) water

method

Wash the rice under the running water until the water runs clear. Drain the rice.

Heat the oil in a pan, add cumin seeds and cinnamon sticks. Stir fry until they turn brown. Add the rice, mixed vegetables, salt and turmeric.

Add water and stir by using a flat spoon.

Bring the water to the boil, and reduce the heat to a low setting. Cover the pan tightly and let it cook for 20 mins, stirring occasionally until the rice is no longer brittle and all the water is absorbed.

Take the pan off the heat.

Gently stir with a flat spoon. Close the lid again, and let the rice sit for 5 to 10 mins.

Transfer into a serving dish and garnish with coriander.

Pilau rice is normally eaten with kadhi sauce.

🏵 Vegetable Biriyani

SERVES 4

PREPARATION TIME 30 MINS   COOKING TIME 60 MINS (INC PILAU RICE)

12oz (340gm) basmati rice
1 small potato *(peeled, cubed & deep fried)*
3 medium mushrooms *(sliced & deep fried)*
1 small onion *(sliced)*
4oz mixed peppers *(sliced or cubed)*
4oz (110gm) cashew nuts *(deep fried)*
4-5 sprigs fresh coriander *(finely chopped for garnish)*
3 tsp desiccated coconut *(for garnish)*
Oil for deep-frying

Sauce:
1 small onion
1 12oz (340gm) tin tomatoes *(liquidised)*
1 tsp ginger *(crushed)*
1 tsp garlic *(crushed)*
1 tsp garam masala
1/2 tsp turmeric
1 tsp cumin and coriander powder
1 tsp chilli powder
10 tbsp cooking oil
1 tsp salt

method for sauce Heat the oil in a pan, add the onions, cook until golden brown. Add the tomatoes and all the spices, let it simmer on a low heat for 5-10 mins stirring frequently.

method for rice Cook the rice as pilau rice (page 77). Deep-fry the potatoes, mushrooms and cashew nuts separately.

Let the rice cool down completely. Transfer into a dish, add potatoes, mushrooms, cashew nuts, pepper, onions and half the fresh coriander, mix well.

Add the sauce and mix again.

Before serving, warm the biriyani in a microwave or in an oven.

Garnish with fresh coriander and coconut.

This biriyani can be eaten on its own, with a salad or moistened to taste with kadhi sauce.

Tip: *Leftover biriyani, mixed with kadhi and eaten with hot buttered toast is divine.*

Coriander Rice

SERVES 4

PREPARATION TIME 30 MINS   COOKING TIME 25 MINS (INC PILAU RICE)

12oz (340gm) basmati rice
½ bunch fresh coriander *(finely chopped)*
1 medium onion *(finely chopped)*
2 tsp cumin seeds
½ tsp garlic *(crushed)*
3 tbsp ghee
2 tsp salt

method

Cook the rice as plain boiled rice.

Let the rice cool completely.

Heat the ghee in a pan, add the cumin seeds, stir fry until brown.

Add garlic, onions and coriander and stir-fry for 1 min.

Add the cooked rice and mix well with a slotted spoon so as not to damage the rice.

Cover the pan and leave it on a very low heat for 5 mins.

Serve with plain yoghurt.

❀ Stir-Fried Rice

Rice dish that is ideal for barbecues.

SERVES 4

PREPARATION TIME 30 MINS   COOKING TIME 25 MINS

12oz (340gm) basmati rice
1 medium onion *(sliced)*
1 red pepper *(sliced and seeded)*
1/4lb (110gm) peas *(defrosted)*
2 carrots *(peeled and julienned)*
3 tbsp sweetcorn kernels *(defrosted)*

2 tsp green chillies *(crushed)*
1 tsp garlic *(crushed)*
3 tbsp oil
6 tbsp soy sauce
2-3 sprigs coriander *(finely chopped for garnish)*
1/2 tsp salt

method

Prepare and cook rice as plain boiled rice.

Let the boiled rice cool completely.

Heat the oil in a wok or pan.

Add onions, peas, peppers, sweetcorn, carrots, salt, green chillies and garlic.

Stir fry until peas are tender. Remove pan from heat.

Add the stir fried vegetables and soy sauce to the boiled rice.

Mix gently with a flat spoon.

Transfer into a serving dish and garnish with chopped coriander.

🏵 Spinach and Sweetcorn Rice

A nice change from plain rice on the dinner table.

SERVES 4

PREPARATION TIME 30 MINS   COOKING TIME 25 MINS

12oz (340gm) basmati rice
Large bunch spinach *(washed drained & finely chopped)*
8oz (225gm) sweetcorn kernels *(frozen)*
1 small potato *(peeled & cut into cubes)*
2 tsp ginger *(crushed)*
2¹/₂ tsp green chillies *(crushed)*

4 cloves
3 cinnamon sticks
¹/₄ lb (110gm) cashew nuts *(deep fried for garnish)*
1 small onion *(chopped into rings & deep fried for garnish)*
3 sprigs coriander *(finely chopped for garnish)*
2 tbsp ghee
1¹/₂ tsp salt

method

Cook the rice as plain boiled rice.

Leave it aside.

Heat the ghee in a pan, add the cloves and cinnamon sticks.

Let the cloves pop and cinnamon change colour.

Add the spinach, ginger, salt, chillies and cook on a low heat for 10-15 mins stirring frequently or until the potatoes are cooked.

Add the sweetcorn kernels and cook for a further 5 mins.

Add the spinach and sweetcorn mix to the cooked rice and mix well.

Transfer into a serving dish, garnish with fried cashew nuts, onion rings and fresh coriander.

Kadhi sauce or plain yoghurt are normally served with this rice.

Hing -
asafoetida
is useful *in*
combatting colic

🏵 Khichadi Rice cooked with daal

SERVES 4

PREPARATION TIME 35 MINS (INC SOAKING)   COOKING TIME 25 MINS

6oz (170gm) basmati rice
6oz (170gm) mung daal *(unshelled)*
1/4 tsp turmeric powder
5 tbsp ghee
1 tsp cumin seeds
3 cloves garlic *(crushed)*
1 1/2 tsp salt
2pts (1.1l) water

method

Soak the daal for 30 mins. (Wash and remove the loose shells and drain).

Wash and drain the rice.

Heat 2 tbsp of ghee in pan, add cumin seeds and let it sizzle until it turns brown. Add the garlic and stir fry.

Add the rice, daal, water, salt and turmeric and mix well.

Bring the water to the boil, lower the heat to very low, close the lid, let it cook for 20-25 mins, stirring gently with a spoon once, until the rice and the daal are no longer brittle and all the water is absorbed.

Add the remaining 3 tbsp of ghee, stir gently and let the khichadi sit for 5-10 mins.

Khichadi is often served with plain yoghurt - or kadhi sauce.

This dish is *ideal* for
someone who is *recovering*
from an illness
or *loss of appetite*

🌼 Maragi Rice

A very popular East African rice recipe, ideal accompaniment to a salad buffet.

SERVES 4

PREPARATION TIME 20 MINS   COOKING TIME 40 MINS

12oz (340g) basmati rice
14oz (400g) tin red kidney beans
1 medium onion *(finely chopped)*
2 tomatoes *(chopped)*
1 red pepper *(sliced)*
1 tsp garlic (*crushed*)
1½ tsp ginger (*crushed*)

2 sticks cinnamon
4 cloves
2 tsp cumin seeds
4-5 green chillies *(halved)*
2-3 sprigs coriander *(finely chopped for garnish)*
3 tbsp oil
2 tsp salt

method

Cook the rice as plain rice.

Wash the kidney beans to remove the salt and set aside.

Heat the oil in a pan and add cinnamon, cumin seeds and cloves.

When sizzled, add onions and cook until golden brown.

Add tomatoes, peppers, ginger, garlic and green chillies. Mix and cook for 10 mins stirring occasionally.

Add the kidney beans and cook for a further 5 mins.

Let the rice cool down completely. Add the kidney bean mixture to the rice and mix well.

Re-heat the rice before serving with coriander garnish.

🌸 Kadhi Spicy creamy yoghurt sauce

Delicious with pilau rice and biriyani. A hot cup of kadhi relieves flu symptoms.

SERVES 4

PREPARATION TIME 20 MINS   COOKING TIME 30 MINS

15oz (425gm) plain yoghurt

3 tsp gram flour

1 tsp garlic *(crushed)*

1 tsp ginger *(crushed)*

1 tsp green chillies *(crushed)*

2 tsp amba hardar *(fresh turmeric)*

or ¼ tsp turmeric powder

2-3 sprigs finely chopped dill *(optional)*

2 tsp cumin seeds

3-4 cloves

10 limdi leaves *(curry leaves)*

½ tsp ghee

2-3 sprigs fresh coriander *(finely chopped for garnish)*

4 tsp sugar

1 tsp salt

½ pt (280ml) water

method

Put yoghurt in a mixing bowl, add gram flour and water and whisk to get rid of the lumps.

Add salt, ginger, garlic, green chillies, sugar and turmeric and mix well.

Heat the ghee in a pan, add cumin and cloves. When browned, add limdi leaves, stir and add the yoghurt mixture.

Keep stirring until the kadhi comes to the boil. Leave to simmer for 5 mins, add chopped dill and remove from the heat.

Garnish with coriander before serving.

🌻 Daal A savoury sauce

Daal sauce is a very popular accompaniment with most meals and rice dishes.

SERVES 4-6

PREPARATION TIME 20 MINS   COOKING TIME 30 MINS

½lb (225gm) tuwer daal *(split pigeon peas)*
2 tsp ginger *(crushed)*
2 tsp green chillies *(crushed)*
2 tsp sugar
½ tsp turmeric powder *(hardar)*
½ tsp hing *(asafoetida)* powder
4-5 dried red chillies
3-4 cloves

1 14oz (400gm) tin tomatoes *(liquidised)*
1 tsp mustard seeds
Juice of 2 lemons
3 tbsp oil
1 tsp salt
2 ¾ pt (1.5l) water
3 sprigs fresh coriander *(finely chopped for garnish)*

method for daal

Soak the tuwer daal for 20 mins, wash and boil in water until tender, then liquidise.

Add ginger, green chillies, salt, turmeric and sugar to the daal and bring to the boil.

In a separate pan, heat the oil and add the mustard seeds and allow it to pop.

Add dried red chillies, cloves and hing and stir well.

Add the mixture to the daal mix and stir well.

Simmer on a low heat for 10-15 mins.

Add the lemon juice.

Daal sauce is used rather like Europeans use gravy.

Garnish with coriander before serving.

Tip: *Keep the kitchen well ventilated to remove the pungent smell when the red chillies and hing are mixed in the pan.*

Cumin seeds -
jeeru are good
for *indigestion*
and *colic*

Coriander - dhania
is good for *headaches*

Breads

Rotli - Chappati   97

Puri   98

Tikhi (Spicy) Puri   98

Khatta Puda   100

Batura   101

Paretha   102

Stuffed Paretha   103

*M*ost Indian breads are made from wheat flour which comes in a variety of different textures, for example: wholemeal has added bran, medium has slightly less and light has almost none.

Always sift the flour before making dough.

There are many varieties of bread and the most common ones are Rotli (chappati), Rotla (millet chappatis), Puri, Batura, Puran Puri and Naan (North India mainly). Again breads can be spicy, salty or stuffed. They can be griddled, shallow or deep fried.

Making the dough varies, depending on which type of bread you are making. Gujarati chappati dough needs boiling hot water for the dough and oil keeps them supple for a long time, even after having gone cold. For Puri's, use cold water and very little oil as it will be fried in oil anyway. Gujarati Rotlis are usually very thin and small in diameter (6 to 8 ins) compared to Rotlis made in the other parts of India .

Wheat flour is extremely nutritious.

Varieties of flour

There is a big selection of flour available for making special, sweet and savoury dishes.

For example:

Urad Daal flour makes papad (papadom).

Rice flour makes pancakes.

Gram flour makes the batter for most fritter-like snacks or pancakes.

Some dishes require a mixture of flours. Many of these are available ready mixed for ease of use,

For example:

> **Dhokhra flour**
>
> **Ondhwo flour**
>
> **Magaj flour** for sweet dishes.
>
> **Mathya flour** for savoury, thin and crispy or deep fried snacks.

✿ Rotli Chapatti - a must for all Gujarati meals

Children love them, hot-off-the-pan with ghee/butter spread on them and sugar sprinkled on top.

MAKES 16-17 chappatis
PREPARATION TIME 15 MINS   COOKING TIME 40 MINS

1lb (450gm) chappati flour *(fine white)*
Ghee or butter *(for brushing on the finished chappatis - optional)*
5 tbsp oil
1 tsp salt
½ pt (280ml) water *(boiling)*

method

Combine the flour, salt and oil in a mixing bowl, blend all the oil into the flour using your fingers.

Using a little water at a time, continue to mix with a spatula until it forms a rough dough. Knead well with your hands.

Use a little oil on your hands and form a smooth dough. The dough should not be too stiff.

Divide the dough into 16-17 portions and form into small balls. Flatten a ball of dough into a 2 inch (50mm) patty and dust both sides with flour. Roll it out evenly into a 6 inch (150mm) diameter chappati, using dusting flour from time to time to avoid it sticking to the rolling surface.

Put the chappati onto a preheated griddle with a slapping action. As soon as bubbles appear turn it over, and let it cook for ½ minute on the other side. Turn it over again and lightly press the chappati with a cloth, to encourage it to puff up.

When the chappatti is slightly brown on both sides, remove it from the griddle, lay it on a tea towel and brush it with a little ghee or butter to keep it soft.

To keep them soft, store the chappatis in an airtight container wrapped in a tea towel.

Tip: *When baking a rotli on the griddle, only half bake the rotli and finish off on the naked gas flame using some form of a rack to avoid burning it on the fierce gas flames. This also makes the rotli baloon up due to the sudden creation of steam on the inside.*

🌸 Puri Deep fried bread

A good alternative to chappatis

MAKES 20 puris
PREPARATION TIME 15 MINS   FRYING TIME 40 MINS

8oz (225gm) chappati flour *(wheat)*
2 tbsp oil
Oil for deep-frying

1 tsp of salt
¹/₄ pt (140ml) water

method

Combine the flour and salt into a mixing bowl. Add oil and salt. Using your finger tips rub the flour until well mixed. Add the water and knead the mixture with your hands until it forms a stiff dough. Take a little oil onto your hands, knead well to form a smooth dough.

Divide the dough into 20 portions and form into smooth balls. Take one ball and roll into a 3¹/₂ inch (85mm) round, on a lightly greased surface.

Heat the oil for deep-frying to a moderately high heat. When the oil is hot, gently slide the puri into the oil, *(see photographs p21)* when the puri comes on to the surface pat it gently with a slotted spoon to encourage it to puff up. Turn it over and fry until golden brown on both sides. Remove from the oil with the slotted spoon onto a paper towel.

Repeat until all puris are made.

Tip: *If the puris come out too oily, the temperature of the oil is too low.*

🌸 Tikhi (Spicy) Puri

A spicy version of the above

MAKES 20 puris
PREPARATION TIME 15 MINS   FRYING TIME 40 MINS

Ingredients as for plain puris plus:

¹/₄ tsp turmeric powder
1tsp ajmo (carom or cumin seeds)

method

Follow the recipe for plain puris but adding the above ingredients when making the dough.

These puris are eaten for breakfast with pickles or plain yoghurt mixed with a little red chilli powder, depending on how spicy you like it.

🌸 Khatta Puda Savoury yoghurt and onion pancake

MAKES 4

PREPARATION TIME 20 MINS   FRYING TIME 30 MINS

7oz (180gm) plain yoghurt
1oz (25gm) gram flour
1oz (25gm) semolina (fine)
2 medium onions *(finely chopped)*
1 tsp chilli *(crushed)*
1 tsp ginger *(crushed)*

¼ bunch coriander *(finely chopped)*
¼ bunch fenugreek *(finely chopped)*
Oil for shallow frying
½ tsp salt
⅛ pt (70ml) water

method

Sieve the gram flour into a large mixing bowl. Add all the ingredients and mix well until the batter is at a pouring consistency.

Heat a fairly thick griddle to a moderate heat (a cast iron frying pan would be ideal).

Pour a tablespoon of oil onto the griddle and grease with a paper towel.

Pour the batter onto the griddle quickly and spread it as thinly as possible with the back of a ladle.

Fry for a minute before turning over, then dribble a teaspoon of oil around the edges and on top of the pancake. Continue frying like this until both sides are golden brown. Pressing the pancake with a spatula during the frying will help it cook evenly.

The pudas are now ready to serve with plain yoghurt or a chutney of your choice.

 Batura

A perfect alternative to naan bread, only better when eaten hot-off-the-pan.

MAKES 20 baturas
PREPARATION TIME 20 MINS   FRYING TIME 40 MINS

1lb (450gm) self raising flour
9oz (255gm) plain yoghurt
1 tbsp of cumin seeds *(roasted and slightly crushed)*
6-7 sprigs fresh fenugreek *(finely chopped - optional)*
2 tsp oil
Oil for deep-frying
1 tsp salt
1 tbsp water

method

Combine the yoghurt, cumin seeds, self-raising flour, oil and fenugreek into a large mixing bowl. With your fingertips blend the ingredients into the flour. Add the water to the flour and form a rough dough, removing all the mixture from the sides of the bowl.

Apply a little oil onto your hands and knead well to form a smooth dough. Cover the bowl with a cloth and let it sit for 5-6 hours in a warm place. The dough should rise and ferment.

Divide the dough into 20 portions forming smooth balls. Roll them into small rounds (4 inches - 100mm) on a lightly greased surface.

Roll a few out and place them onto a cloth.

Heat the oil to a moderately high heat in a karai, wok or deep fat fryer. When the oil is hot, gently slide the batura into the oil.

When the batura comes up to the surface, gently pat with a slotted spoon, to encourage it to puff up.

Turn it over and let it fry for a few seconds. Turn it over again and remove it from the oil and lay it on a paper towel. The bread should be a pale colour but not brown.

🌸 Paretha Shallow fried unleavened bread

MAKES 9 paretha

PREPARATION TIME 15 MINS   COOKING TIME 45 MINS

Dough as for chapattis (p85)   1 tsp of salt
1lb (450gm) chappati flour *(wheat)*   ¹/₂ pt (280ml) hot water
5 tbsp of oil

method

Make the dough as for chappati dough. Divide the dough into 9 large portions. Roll them into 6 inch (150mm) rounds. Try not to make them too thin.

Brush oil onto the rolled chappati and sprinkle some dry flour on top. To create layers in the paretha, lift the top edge and roll it into a tight tube. Form the tube into a spiral wheel shape on a lightly floured surface. Form the spiral wheel into a smooth ball again. Roll out the ball into a 5 inch (150mm) round by applying even pressure, on a lightly floured surface.

method for frying

Pre-heat the griddle to a moderate heat. Place the paretha on the griddle and cook for 30 secs. Turn it over then dribble a teaspoon of oil around the edges and on top of the paretha. Continue frying like this until both sides are golden brown. Pressing the paretha with a spatula during the frying will help it to cook evenly.

🦁 Stuffed Paretha

MAKES 10
PREPARATION TIME 30 MINS   COOKING TIME 90 MINS

Dough as for chapattis (p85)
Stuffing:
2 large potatoes *(boiled and mashed to a smooth texture)*
1 medium onion *(finely chopped)*
2¹/₂ tsp green chillies *(crushed)*
2-3 sprigs of fresh coriander *(finely chopped)*
1 tsp sugar
1¹/₂ tsp salt
¹/₄ tsp cinnamon powder
Juice of ¹/₂ lemon

method

Add all the stuffing ingredients to the mashed potato and mix well. Divide the mixture and the dough into 10 balls each.

Roll out the dough into a round shape (5in/125mm) on a lightly floured surface and put the mixture in the centre. Bring in the edges to seal in the mixture and make into a flattened ball shape.

Dip it into some dry flour and roll gently into a thick round about 6in (150mm) diameter.

To fry the paretha follow the frying instructions for plain paretha.

Bitter Gourd - *karela*
— the juice of this
vegetable if *drunk*
regularly helps to
combat *diabetes*

Kachumbar – Salads, Raitas and Pickles

Green Mixed Salad   106

Raita   110

Cucumber Raita   110

Onion and Tomato Salad   109

Onion Salad in Tomato Ketchup   109

Sambharo – Stir-fried cabbage   111

Fresh Apple Pickle   112

Carrot and Green Chilli Pickle   112

Keri-no-Chundo – Raw Mango Preserve   113

*M*ost Indian salads are a combination of one, two or more different types of salad vegetables and fruits, such as tomatoes, cucumber, lettuce, radish, onion, pepper and mura (muli) only.

The most common seasoning and dressing used in Indian salads are lemon juice, yoghurt, roasted cumin, salt and chillies. Salads are called Kachumbar.

Pickles come in many varieties, textures and strengths. The main ingredients of most pickles are crushed fenugreek and mustard seeds, chillies, gor (jaggery) and oil. A ready mixed base is available, just add oil and your own choice of vegetables and fruits.

Many vegetables and fruits can be pickled, depending on their texture, as ones with a mushy texture will not last long, eg apples.

A pickle tray is a must at a Gujarati dinner table. Pickles are eaten as an accompaniment to the main meal. You will see a pickle tray at breakfast time too. Sweet pickles are especially eaten with leftover rotlis (chappatis) which are shallow fried (see leftover section), parethas and spicy puris.

Some varieties of fruits and vegetables are dried under the hot sun before pickling.

🌸 Green Mixed Salad

SERVES 4

PREPARATION AND MIXING TIME 20 MINS

½ cucumber *(finely chopped)*
1 small red onion *(finely chopped)*
2 carrots *(grated)*
½ lettuce *(chopped)*
5 radishes *(finely chopped)*
2 tomatoes *(finely chopped)*
1 tsp cumin *(roasted & lightly crushed)*
2-3 sprigs fresh coriander *(finely chopped for garnish)*
Juice of 1 lemon
1 fresh lemon *(cut into wedges for garnish)*
½ tsp salt

method

Mix all the ingredients into a bowl except for the lettuce.

Spread the lettuce onto a serving bowl or dish, and lay the salad mixture on top.

Garnish with lemon wedges.

Tip: *Lime and coriander dressing, available from most supermarkets, goes well with this salad.*

 Raita

SERVES 4–6

PREPARATION AND MIXING TIME 20 MINS

½ cucumber *(finely chopped)*

1 small onion *(finely chopped)*

2 carrots *(grated)*

½ red pepper *(finely cubed)*

1½ cartons *(22.5 oz/625gm)* plain yoghurt

2 tsp cumin *(roasted & lightly crushed)*

1 tsp fennel seeds *(lightly crushed)*

2½ tsp sugar

2-3 sprigs fresh coriander *(finely chopped for garnish)*

½ tsp salt *(to taste)*

method

Mix all the ingredients in a bowl.

Transfer into a serving bowl and garnish with coriander.

 Cucumber Raita

SERVES 4

PREPARATION AND MIXING TIME 20 MINS

1 cucumber *(unpeeled)*

½ tsp split mustard seeds

½ tsp green chillies *(crushed)*

Small pinch of turmeric powder

1 carton *(15 oz/425gm)* plain yoghurt

2-3 sprigs of coriander *(finely chopped for garnish)*

1 tsp salt

1½ tsp sugar

method

Grate all the cucumber and squeeze all the water out.

Place the cucumber in a bowl, add the rest of the ingredients. Mix well.

Transfer into a serving dish and refrigerate.

Garnish with coriander before serving.

❀ Onion and Tomato Salad

SERVES 4–6
PREPARATION AND MIXING TIME 10 MINS

2 small onions *(sliced into thin rings)*
¹/₂ lb (225gm) tomatoes *(sliced)*
5-6 sprigs of coriander *(finely chopped for garnish)*

2 tsp cumin seeds *(roasted & lightly crushed)*
Juice of 1 lemon
1 tsp salt

method Mix onions and tomatoes together in a bowl. Add the rest of the ingredients and mix well again.

Arrange it on a serving plate garnished with the coriander.

❀ Onion Salad in Tomato Ketchup

SERVES 4
PREPARATION AND MIXING TIME 10 MINS

1 medium onion *(thinly sliced)*
4 tsp tomato ketchup

¹/₂ tsp salt
1 tsp chilli powder

method Soak the sliced onions for 5 mins in warm water to remove the sharpness and drain.

Add the rest of the ingredients to the onions and mix well.

Sambharo Stir fried cabbage, carrot and chilli seed

SERVES 4

PREPARATION TIME 20 MINS   COOKING TIME 10 MINS

1½ lb (675gm) cabbage *(shredded)*
2 medium carrots *(peeled & grated)*
15 green chillies *(halved lengthways)*
or 1 green pepper *(thinly sliced)*
2 tsp mustard seeds
Juice of ½ lemon
¼ tsp turmeric powder
3 tbsp oil
1¼ tsp salt
Lettuce *(to serve)*

method   Heat the oil to a high heat in a wok or frying pan. Add mustard seeds, when popped add cabbage, carrots and chillies. Add turmeric and salt and mix well.

Cover pan and cook the mixture on a low heat for 8-10 mins stirring frequently.

Remove pan from the heat, add the lemon juice and mix well. Serve on a bed of lettuce.

🌹 Fresh Apple Pickle

This recipe can also be used for fresh mangoes, gooseberries and carrots.

SERVES 4-6

PREPARATION AND MIXING TIME 20 MINS

2 cooking apples

2 tsp fenugreek seeds *(crushed)*

2 tsp mustard seeds *(crushed)*

1 tsp chilli powder *(more if you prefer it hot)*

Juice of one lemon

2 tsp sugar

1 tsp salt

2-3 tbsp oil

If using ready mixed fenugreek and mustard mix available from Asian grocery shops, use 4 tsps of mixture, in place of all the ingredients except for the apples, the lemon juice and the oil.

method
Slice the apples into thin wedges. Do not slice the apples too much in advance. This avoids discolouration of the apples. Mix the apple wedges with the rest of the ingredients, in a bowl

It is now ready to serve. It keeps for two days if refrigerated.

🌹 Carrot and Green Chilli Pickle

SERVES 4

PREPARATION AND MIXING TIME 20 MINS

2 carrots *(peeled & julienned)*

10 green chillies *(halved)*

2 tsp mustard seeds

1/2 tsp chilli powder

Juice of 1 lemon

2 tbsp oil

1/2 tsp salt

method
Heat the oil in a pan and add the mustard seeds. Once they have popped, remove pan from heat and add the oil to the carrot and chillies. Add the rest of the ingredients and mix well.

It is now ready to serve and will stay fresh for two days.

🦁 Keri-no-Chhundo Green mango preserve

A preserve made from unripe mangoes.

SERVES 4-6
PREPARATION TIME 20 MINS   COOKING TIME 40 MINS

6 small green mangos	5 cloves
1½ tsp chilli powder	7 tbsp oil
5 sticks cinnamon	6 tbsp sugar
3 cardamon pods	1 tsp salt

method

Wash peel and grate the mangoes. To avoid discolouration, mix the grated mangoes in salt and leave to one side.

Heat the oil in a pan, add cinnamon, cardamon and cloves. When they sizzle add the mangoes and cook the mixture on a low heat stirring continuously for 30 mins until the liquid has evaporated and a thick syrup remains. Add the sugar.

Remove from heat and leave to cool.

Add chilli powder and store in an air-tight jar and refrigerate. This preserve should last 2-3 weeks.

Delicious with spicy puri.

Cinnamon - taj is good for *colds,* coughs, asthma *and* nausea

Desserts

Gulab Jambu   117

Gajjar Halwa   119

Shirkand   121

Sev – Vermicelli   122

Seero – Semolina   123

Lapsi – Bulgar wheat   125

Gujaratis are well known for their sweet tooth. Most of the desserts are extra sweet, but could be made to suit your own taste by trial and error. The sweet meats are served first or together with the main course meal. The Ayurvedic explanation for this is that eating something sweet at the beginning of the meal enlivens the taste buds and therefore the rest of the food would taste that much better.

On a more social note, a sweet offering is made at the beginning of a meal to ensure that the interaction during the course of the meal would remain 'just as sweet and friendly.'

Gujarati sweet shops are full of vividly coloured offerings, some spherical (Ladoos), some small cubes (Barfis), some bright orangy curly swirls (Jalebis) and some in semi liquid form (Kheers). Some have a pure silver covering, microns thick and edible, just for decoration purposes.

Ladoos – usually use gram flour mixed with sugar and ghee as a base to which other ingredients such as pistachio, almonds, dried fruit, coconut, colouring, etc. are added to vary the taste and texture .

Barfis – this fudge like sweet uses milk powder and sugar as a base to which ingredients similar to those used in the ladoos are used for the same effects .

Shrikands – are very popular desserts which are similar to fruit yoghurts but with sweet spices that give them a uniquely Indian flavour .

Lapsi, Seero and Sev – these are hot sweets made with boiled bulgar wheat, semolina or fine vermicelli, respectively, as a base. Again sultanas, almonds and pistachio nuts are used to vary its taste and textures .

Kheers – are basically milk puddings where rice (plain or flattened) or vermicelli are used, garnished with sweet spices for flavourings .

Keri-no-Raas – (Mango pulp) is also a very popular accompaniment to a meal, but it is seasonal .

🌹 Gulab Jambu Most common Indian dessert

SERVES 10

PREPARATION TIME 40 MINS   COOKING TIME 3¹/₂ HOURS (INC 2 HOURS SOAKING TIME)

¹/₂ lb (225gm) milk powder
2oz (57gm) semolina *(fine)*
¹/₂ tbsp ghee
¹/₂ tsp baking powder
¹/₂ tsp cardamon seeds *(crushed for garnish)*
³/₈ pt (200ml) milk
Oil for deep frying

For the syrup:
1¹/₄ lb (560gm) sugar
¹/₂ pt (280ml) water
Pinch of saffron

method Mix the milk powder, baking powder, ghee and cardamon in a bowl. With your hands blend the mixture together for 10 mins, then leave aside.

Add the semolina to the milk in a bowl and let it soak and do not stir for 10 mins.

Add the semolina mixture to the milk powder mixture. Mix well and knead for half an hour until a smooth dough forms.

Divide the dough into 45 tiny portions.

Roll each portion into smooth balls applying gentle pressure.

Heat the oil, on a low heat, and deep fry the balls, a few at a time, until golden brown.

Remove and allow to cool.

method for syrup Mix the sugar and saffron into the water and let it boil on a low heat for 40 mins, stirring the water once or twice, then let it cool.

When the syrup and balls are both cold, add the balls into the syrup and gently mix until the balls are completely soaked by the syrup.

Let the balls soak for 2 hours to absorb the syrup.

Serve hot or cold with desiccated coconut and crushed cardamon for garnish.

Tips: *Gulab Jambus freeze really well in a sealed container. Defrost before serving.*

❀ Gajjar Halwa

SERVES 4
PREPARATION TIME 15 MINS   COOKING TIME 40 MINS

1 1/2 lb (675gm) carrots *(peeled & grated)*
2 tbsp ghee
3/8 pt (200ml) milk
2oz (57gm) milk powder
1/2 tsp cardamon seeds *(crushed)*
15 sultanas
2oz (57gm) sugar

For Garnish
1 tsp pistachios *(slivered)*
2 tbsp desiccated coconut
3 almonds *(slivered)*

method

Heat the ghee in a pan, add carrots, stir fry at a low heat until all the liquid is absorbed and the ghee becomes visible on the surface.

Add milk, continue to stir fry until all the milk is absorbed.

Add sugar and mix well. Continue to cook at a low heat until the sugar is absorbed completely. Remove from the heat when the mixture starts to stick to the bottom of the pan.

Let the mixture cool for 10 mins.

Add the milk powder, mix well and spread the mixture into a baking tray about 6 inch (150mm) diameter or square and 1 inch (25mm) deep.

Smooth the mixture with a spatula and garnish.

When the mixture is set cut into 4 pieces.

Serve hot with cream or ice-cream.

❀ Shrikand A Gujarati speciality whipped yoghurt dessert

SERVES 4-6

PREPARATION AND MIXING TIME 30 MINS (EXCLUDING DRAINING TIME)

30oz (850gm) yoghurt *(plain)*
6oz (175gm) sugar
1 tsp cardamon seeds *(crushed)*
1 tsp pistachio nuts *(crushed)*
11oz (300gm) mandarins *(or any other fruit of your choice - drained)*

method

Tie the yogurt in a muslin (cheescloth) cloth and place it in a colander.

Place the colander in a large bowl and leave to drain for 9-10 hours. The yogurt will now be reduced to a thick curd.

Transfer the curd into a bowl, add sugar, stir lightly and leave to stand for 20 mins.

Beat the mixture until it is light and smooth, add the fruit and $1/2$ tsp cardamon to the mixture and mix gently to avoid damaging the fruit.

Transfer to a serving dish and garnish with some fruit, the rest of the cardamon and pistachios. Refrigerate before serving.

Tips: *Shrikand can be made in advance and stored in a fridge for up to 2-3 days, without the fruit garnish.*

Shrikand can also be frozen for up to 1 month without the garnish and the fruit. Defrost by leaving it out for 3-4 hours before serving with the garnish.

🦁 Sev - Vermicelli

SERVES 2

PREPARATION TIME 10 MINS   COOKING TIME 30 MINS

8oz (225gm) sev *(vermicelli)*
2 tbsp ghee
2 tsp cardomon seeds *(crushed)*
10 sultanas
3 almonds *(slivered for garnish)*
3-4 pistachios *(slivered for garnish)*
8oz (225gm) sugar
2 pts (1.2l) boiling water

method

Heat the ghee in a pan, on a low heat, add sev and stir fry until golden brown.

Add the boiling water, stir well and cover the pan. Continue to cook, stirring occasionally, until all the water is absorbed.

Add sugar, sultanas and cardamon and mix well. Continue to cook until all the liquid formed from the sugar is absorbed.

Transfer into a serving dish and garnish with almonds and pistachios.

Serve hot.

🦁 Seero – Semolina

SERVES 2

PREPARATION TIME 10 MINS   COOKING TIME 30 MINS

¹/₄ lb (110gm) semolina *(fine)*
2 tbsp ghee
10 sultanas
¹/₄ pt (140ml) boiling water *(boil with a pinch of saffron)*
2oz (50gm) sugar
3-4 pistachio nuts *(slivered)*
2 tsp cardamon seeds *(crushed)*
Pinch of saffron

method

Heat the ghee in a pan then lower the heat and add the semolina. Stir fry until the semolina turns golden brown then add the sultanas and boiling water whilst continuing to stir.

Stir until the semolina starts to stick to the bottom of the pan.

Add sugar and 1 tsp of cardamon, stir then cover the pan and let it cook for a further 15-20 mins until all the sugar is absorbed.

Transfer the semolina into a dish and garnish with cardamon, almonds and pistachio.

Can be served hot or cold.

🦁 Lapsi - Bulgar wheat

SERVES 2

PREPARATION TIME 10 MINS   COOKING TIME 30 MINS

¼ lb (110gm) lapsi *(bulgar wheat, fine)*
2 tbsp ghee
2 tsp cardamon seeds *(crushed)*
3 sticks cinnamon
6-7 sultanas
1 tsp of fennel seeds
2-3 almonds *(slivered for garnish)*
2-3 pistachios *(slivered for garnish)*
1 tbsp desiccated coconut *(for garnish)*
4oz (110gm) sugar
¾ pt (420ml) boiling water

method

Heat the ghee in a pan and add cinnamon sticks. Let them sizzle until the cinnamon changes to a golden brown colour.

Add lapsi and stir fry until golden brown then add water and cover, stirring occasionally, until the lapsi is no longer brittle, and all the water has been absorbed. Add sugar, fennel seeds and sultanas and mix well.

Let it cook for a further 10 mins or until all the water from the sugar is fully absorbed.

Transfer to a serving dish and garnish with almonds, pistachios and desiccated coconut before serving.

Ginger - aadu
is useful
for *coughs* and
colds

Chai-Pani - Drinks

Sweet Lassi   128

Salty Lassi   128

Mango Lassi   129

Masala-wari Chai - Spicy tea   131

Aadu-wari Chai - Ginger tea   131

Fudna-wari Chai - Mint tea   131

*I*t is quite customary to offer a glass of water to guests to express your hospitality before any interaction commences. In the West this has probably been largely replaced by a soft drink.

Most Gujaratis would start off their day with a cup of masala chai (tea). I personally think that it is the most invigorating drink of the day, warming you from inside out, particularly if you are feeling down or have a headache or flu.

The two most popular drinks at meal times are water and lassi, a thin yoghurt drink. Water is an excellent form of cleanser and yoghurt helps with the digestion of the food.

Tea or coffee is not usually drunk after a meal.

Sweet Lassi

15oz (425gm) plain yoghurt
3-4 tbsp sugar or honey *(to taste)*
1½tsp fennel seeds *(crushed)*
¾ pt (420ml) water

method
Mix the yoghurt and water in a large container and whisk to a fine consistency. Add the sugar and half the fennel and stir well.

Transfer into a serving jug and refrigerate.

Before serving, stir well and garnish with the rest of the fennel seeds.

Salty Lassi

15oz (425gm) plain yoghurt
2 tsp roasted cumin seeds *(crushed)*
2 sprigs fresh coriander *(finely chopped for garnish)*
2 tbsp salt *(to taste)*
¾ pt (420ml) water

method
Mix the yoghurt and water in a large container and whisk to a fine consistency. Add the salt and half the cumin seeds and stir well.

Transfer into a serving jug and refrigerate.

Before serving, stir well and garnish with the rest of the cumin seeds and coriander.

Mango Lassi

15oz (425gm) plain yoghurt
10 tbsp mango pulp
sugar (optional)
3/4 pt (420ml) water

method   Mix the yoghurt and water in a large container and whisk to a fine consistency. Add the mango pulp and stir well.

Transfer into a serving jug and refrigerate.

 Masala-wari Chai Spicy tea

¹/₄pt (140ml) milk *(optional)*
1¹/₂ tsp tea leaves or 2 teabags
¹/₂ tsp chai masala *(to taste)*
Sugar *(to taste)*
1pt (560ml) water

method Put all the ingredients in a sauce pan, except for the milk, and bring to the boil. Let it simmer for a minute then add the milk. Bring to the boil again and let it simmer for 3 mins at a low heat.
Pour into a cup using a tea strainer.

Chai masala is readily available in many Asian grocery shops but does vary enormously from manufacturer to manufacturer, so please buy only the smallest packet until you find the one that you lIke the best.

Aadu-wari Chai Ginger tea

Fudna-wari Chai Mint tea

The same recipe as the one above can be used for making ginger tea or mint tea except that the Chai Masala is replaced by freshly grated ginger (1 inch (25mm) root ginger) or fresh mint (6/8 leaves), respectively.

Masala and Ginger can also be used together in the Tea.

All these teas are very good as a 'pick-me-up' drink, especially when suffering from flu symptoms.

🌸 Leftovers

Unlike in the West, we Indians traditionally always cook a little extra, enough for second helpings and enough for unexpected guests. It would be rude not to invite any guests to the dining table if they were to arrive at or around meal times. This obviously means that there will always be leftovers. Gujarati women have managed to create some delicious recipes using the leftovers, a few of which I have mentioned in this section. Please feel free to try some suggestions. No measurements are given as the portions will depend upon the amount of food left over. A lot of experimentation is needed here to achieve a meal to suit your taste.

Leftover Rotlis – chapattis:

Bean Rolls in cheese

Sauté some onions in oil, add garlic, mixed herbs, oregano, chillies (optional) and salt to taste. Add a tin of baked beans and let it simmer for a minute.

Roll a couple of tbsp of this stuffing in a rotli and place in a suitable baking tray or dish. Make as many bean rolls as required and sprinkle plenty of grated cheese, of your choice, on the bean rolls. Bake the rolls for 5-10 mins in a preheated oven or a microwave oven.

Serve the rolls with salad and sour cream.

Rotli Bake

Break up the leftover rotlis into small pieces in a large bowl and mix them with plain yoghurt. Heat 2 tbsp of oil in a separate pan and add some mustard seeds to it. When the seeds have popped add the yoghurt and rotli mix together with ginger, garlic, crushed green chillies, some shredded cabbage and salt to taste. Mix well and spread the mixture in a baking tray. Bake for 15-20 mins at a medium heat.

Crispy Fried Rotli

Leftover rotli can be shallow fried in a frying pan until it goes crispy brown and, served with yoghurt or pickles it tastes divine.

Leftover Curries:

Dry curries make excellent fillings for toasties and sandwiches.

Wet curries make delicious pie fillings and bakes. Just put the curry in a suitable baking tray, cover with grated cheese or pastry and bake for 15-20 mins and you have a meal and a half.

Leftover Rice:

Fried Rice Balls

My favourite rice recipe is to mix the rice with mashed potato, a little gram flour, ginger, crushed green chillies, chopped onions, fresh coriander and salt to taste. Form small balls with the mixture and deep fry until golden brown. Serve with ketchup or the chutney of your choice.

Leftover Wet Curry and Rice:

My husband's favourite is to mix the curry and rice and heat in the microwave oven and eat with hot buttered toast and salad.

🏵 Medicinal properties of Indian food items

Aadu	*Fresh ginger* - useful for poor appetite, indigestion, coughs and colds.
Ajmo / ajwain	*Carom seeds* - useful for indigestion and abdominal distention.
Amli	*Tamarind pulp* - useful for loss of appetite, thirst, heart problems and nausea.
Bhindi / bhinda	*Ladies fingers* - aphrodisiac, increases lactation, corrects constipation. Not advisable for asthmatics.
Bengal gram	*Black chickpeas* - stimulant, aphrodisiac, good for joint pains.
Channa	*Chickpeas* - nutritious, astringent.
Dhania	*Coriander* - reduces sexual desire.
Elaychi	*Cardamom* - used in combating vomiting, heart disease, suppression of urine and thirst.
Hardar	*Turmeric powder* - an antiseptic. Useful for skin problems, ulcers, wounds, diabetes and bleeding disorders.

Hing	*Asafoetida* - useful in intestinal colic, toothache, abdominal distention, alcoholism.
Jaifer	*Nutmeg* - used when suffering from poor sleep or diarrhoea.
Jeeru	*Cumin seeds* - used for indigestion, colic, diarrhoea, loss of breast milk.
Kadi Patta (Limdo)	*Curry leaves* - useful for digestion, flatulence, distention and dysentery.
Kakadi	*Cucumber* - useful in combating burning urination and kidney disease.
Karela	*Bitter Gourd* - the juice of this vegetable, taken regularly helps to combat diabetes.
Lassun	*Garlic* - used for joint pains, paralysis, painful periods and coughs.
Laving	*Cloves* - clove oil applied externally for toothache, sciatica or joint pains and headaches.
Marcha	*Chillies* - useful for indigestion, joint disorders, dog bite wounds. It is also a poor sexual stimulant.

Mattar	*Garden peas* - fresh peas are a good source of proteins but dry or preserved peas cause flatulence and are heavy to digest.	Rai	*Mustard seeds* - used for skin disorders, poor appetite and intestinal worms.
Methi	*Fenugreek seeds* - used for indigestion, colic, inflammation, body aches, joint pains and diabetes.	Rajma	*Red kidney beans/cow peas* - nutritious, promote urination, good tonic when taken once a week.
Methi	*Fenugreek leaves* - useful for diabetes, liver disorders and joint pains.	Ringan	*Aubergine, egg plant* - useful in combating fever and ease of digestion during loss of appetite.
Muli (Muro)	*Radish* - useful for urinary and liver disorders, urinary stones, oedema and constipation.	Suwa	*Dill seeds* - used to stop vomiting, indigestion, intestinal colic and nausea.
Mung / (Maag)	*Green grams* - light food, easy to digest, useful in fever, diarrhoea, promote good eye-sight, correct constipation.	Taj	*Cinnamon* - useful for colds, coughs, asthma and nausea.
Mushrooms	Rich source of proteins, nutrients and an aphrodisiac.	Taj Patta	*Cinnamon leaves* - useful in intestinal colic, piles and diabetes.
Palak (Bhaji)	*Spinach* - a rich source of Iron, increases urine, corrects constipation, useful in jaundice, during pregnancy, and respiratory distress.	Urad	*Black gram* - very good source of proteins, aphrodisiac, useful for correcting constipation.
		Variyari	*Fennel seeds* - useful in nausea, period pains, indigestion and colic.

Glossary

Aadu	Ginger	Gajjar	Carrots
Ajmo	Carom seeds or Bishop's Seeds	Ghee	Purified butter
Amli	Tamarind	Gor	Jaggery or raw sugar
Athanu	Pickle	Gram	Chick pea or lentil
Atto	Flour	Gulab jambu	Milk powder balls in syrup
Badaam	Almonds	Guwar	Arrow shaped green
Bajri	Millet		vegetable runner bean
Barfi	Indian Fudge	Hardar	Turmeric
Batura	Deep fried yoghurty bread	Halwa	Fudge like dessert
Besan	Gram flour	Hing	Asafetida
Bhaji	Spinach	Idli	Steamed rice dumplings
Bhajiya	Fritters	Jeera	Cumin
Bhinda	Okra, ladies fingers	Juwar	Barley
Chaat	Savoury snack	Kachori	Thin crusted spicy pie
Chai	Tea	Kadhai	Deep frying pan
Channa	Chickpea	Kaju	Cashew nuts
Chevdo	Bombay mix	Kanda	Onions
Chokha	Rice, Chawal	Kara Mari	Black pepper seed
Chora	Black-eyed beans	Karela	Bitter gourd
Chori	Red mung-like bean	Keri	Mango
Cobis	Cabbage	Kesar	Saffron
Daal	Split bean or pulse	Kheer	Rice pudding
Dahi Vada	Daal dumpling in yoghurt	Khichadi	Rice cooked with daal
	sauce	Kofta	Deep fried vegetable or
Dhana	Coriander seeds		daal balls
Dhania	Fresh coriander	Lal Marcha	Red chilli
Dhokhra	Steamed savoury rice cake	Lapsi	Bulgar wheat
Dhosa	Pancake	Lassun	Garlic
Dudhi	Bottle gourd	Lassi	Yoghurt drink (butter milk)
Elaychi	Cardamom	Laving	Cloves
Fudno	Mint	Lila Marcha	Green chillies
Ful Cobi	Cauliflower	Lili Hardar	Fresh turmeric

Limdi	Curry leaves	Sambhar	Vegetable daal sauce
Maag	Mung beans	Seero	Semolina dessert
Maag-ni-daal	Split mung beans	Seragwo	Drumstick
Makai	Corn	Sev	Savoury gram flour noodles
Mamra	Puffed rice	Sev	Vermicelli
Marcha	Chilli	Shak	Curry
Masala	Mixture of spices or stuffing	Shrikhand	Yoghurt dessert
Masoor	Lentils	Soji	Semolina
Mattar	Peas	Suwa	Dill
Mendo	Plain flour	Taj	Cinnamon
Methi	Fenugreek seeds	Tal	Sesame
Methi-ni-bhaji	Fresh fenugreek leaves	Tameta	Tomato
Muth	Mung like brown beans	Tavi	Griddle
Nariyal	Coconut	Thali	Platter *(usually stainless steel)*
Nimakh	Salt		
Paneer	Indian vegetarian cheese	Turya	Ridged gourd
Pani	Water	Tuwer	Pigeon peas
Papad	Papadom	Tuwer daal	Split pigeon peas
Paretha	Unleavened fried bread	Tuwer-ni-sing	Pigeon peas in pod
Patra	Colocassia leaves	Urad	Black mung-like beans
Pilau	Vegetable rice	Vada	Deep fried daal dumplings
Pista	Pistachio nuts	Valor	Indian runner beans
Puri	Deep fried bread		
Puwa	Flattened rice		
Ragdo	Thick sauce		
Rai	Mustard seeds		
Raita	Cucumber and yoghurt relish		
Rajma	Red kidney beans		
Ras Malai	Whey balls in milk		
Ravaiya	Stuffed vegetables		
Ringan	Aubergine		
Rotli	Chappati		

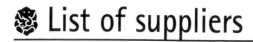

List of suppliers

Kishan Stores
20 Carlton Terrace
East Ham
London E7

Mina Stores
274 Green Street
East Ham
London E7

Kwality Foods
166 Goldhawk Road
East Ham
London W12

Sara Fresh
7 Hereford Road
East Ham
London W2

Bharat Food Stores
Carlton Terracce
East Ham
London E7

Toor Stores
160B High Street North
East Ham
London E7

Toor Stores
8 Queens Market
East Ham
London E13

Sira Cash and Carry
128 The Broadway
Southall
London W9

Quality Food Stores
99 Greenford Avenue
Southall
London W9

Quality Stores
6 The Vale
Acton
London W3

VB and Sons
736 Kenton Road
Kingsbury
London NW9

VB and Sons
147 Ealing Road
Alperton
London HA0

Fruity Fresh
133-135 Ealing Road
Wembley
London W12

Shanta Foods
194 Ealing Road
Wembley
London W12

Pick and Save
29 Goldhawk Road
Kenton
London W12

Mandalia Cash & Carry
287 Burnt Oak
Broadway
Edgware
London

Top-Op Foods
Garland Road (EW)
Stanmore
London

Jaya Karir
42 Regency Court
Brentwood

Ashton Sweet Mart
(ASM)
Oldham Road
Ashton-u-Lyne

Jalaram Food Stores
46 Showell Green Lane
Sparkhill
Birmingham

Mehta Sunderies
329 Shafts Moor Lane
Hall Green
Birmingham

Rani Superstores
728 Stratford Road
Sparkhill
Birmingham

Heathfield
Supermarket
212 Heathfield Road
Hansworth
Birmingham
B19 1JQ

Yogi Supermarket
Stratford Road
Sparkhill
Birmingham

Masaka General
Stores
Stratford Road
Sparkbrook
Birmingham

Surnar & Son
1719 -1721 Coventry
Road
Birmingham

Jays Supermarket
21 Pound Street
Birmingham

Michaels Food Stores
117 Hob Mode Road
95 Ravenhills Road
732-736 Yarleywood Rd
Birmingham

Bharti Spices
Deane Road
Bolton

Raja Penny Profit
220 Deane Road
Bolton

Ahmed Foods
1378 Leeds Road
Bradford 3

Pakeeza Superstores
White Abbey Road
Bradford 3

M.P. Patel and Sons
Arncliffe Terrace
Bradford 7

Lal & Sons
Midland Supermarket
Stoney Stanton Road
Coventry CV1

Sandhu Supermarket
Foreshill Road
Coventry CV6

Cost Cutters
High Street
Leamington Spa

Londis (Royals)
Groceries
Thatch Brooke Road
Leamington Spa

Continental
Supermarket
125 Chapeltown Road
Leeds 8

Continental Food Stores
69-71 Brudnell Grove
Leeds 6

Jalpur Millers
137A Harrison Road
Leicester

Madhur's Krooners
307 St. Saviour Road
Leicester

Kisen Mill
23 Melrose Street
Leicester

Shiva Shakti Foods
McDonald Road
Leicester

Nayik Foods
Unit 7
Tithe Street
Leicester

Ghelani Bros
16 Harrison Street
Leicester

Virpur Millers
272 Harrison Road
Leisester

Apna Cash and Carry
Catherine Road
Northampton

Madina Food Stores
Ratford Road
Hyson Green
Nottingham

Mogul Food Stores
Ratford Road
Hyson Green
Nottingham

Tropical Food Stores
Ratford Road
Hyson Green
Nottingham

Anita Traders
Manley Road
Oldham

Suresh Pau-Raghu
Stores
Gainsborough Avenue
Oldham

Shah Oriental Groceries
451- 453 Abeydale
Sheffield 7

Shafi Supermarket
68 Spital Hill
Sheffield 2

Patel Brothers
Mill Road
Wellingborough

 # Index

A

Aadu, 126, 134, 136
Aadu-wari, 127, 131
Abdominal, 134
Aches, 135
Africa, 8
African, 13, 91
Ageing, 78
Ailments, 13
Ajmo, 22-23, 26, 36, 59, 67, 71-72, 98, 134, 136
Ajwain, 134
Alcoholism, 134
Almonds, 116, 119, 122, 125, 136
Amba, 92
Amli, 134, 136
Antiseptic, 76, 134
Aphrodisiac, 134-135
Apple, 105, 112
Appliances, 18
Asafoetida, 52, 72, 88, 93, 134
Athanu, 136
Atto, 136
Aubergines, 30, 56, 63, 65, 67, 134
Ayurveda, 13

B

Badaam, 136
Bajri, 136
Balti, 20
Banana, 30
Barbecues, 86
Barfis, 115-116, 136
Bark, 23
Barley, 136
Basmati, 78, 80, 83, 85, 89, 91
Bateta, 47, 50, 57, 64
Batura, 77, 95, 101, 136
Belan, 21
Bengal, 134

Besan, 136
Bhaat, 79
Bhagat, 69, 75
Bhaji, 57, 60, 135, 136
Bhajiyas, 10, 27, 29, 43, 69, 136
Bhel, 41
Bhinda, 134, 136
Bhindi, 134
Bicarbonate, 35, 54
Biriyani, 79, 83, 92
Black-eyed, 51, 71, 136
Bran, 95
Breads, 8, 10, 16-17, 20-21, 27, 29, 95-98, 100-103, 136-137
Breakfast, 9, 27, 47, 105
Breast, 134
Brine, 69
Bulgar, 115-116, 125, 136
Butter, 80, 97, 133, 136

C

Cabbage, 57, 61, 105, 111, 132, 136
Caraway, 22
Carbohydrates, 57
Cardamon, 22-23, 113, 117, 119-120, 122-123, 125, 134, 136
Carom, 22-23, 26, 36, 59, 67, 71-72, 134, 136
Carrots, 34, 41, 44, 52, 57, 81, 86, 105, 106, 108, 111, 119, 136
Cashew, 83, 87, 136
Cauliflower, 30, 57-58, 136
Chaat, 41, 136
Chai, 23, 127, 131, 136
Chai-pani, 127
Channa, 47, 50, 69, 73, 75, 134, 136
Chappatis, 16-17, 21, 58, 78, 95, 97-98, 102-103, 105, 132, 137

Chawal, 136
Cheescloth, 120
Cheese, 132-133, 137
Chevdo, 136
Chick, 49-50, 136
Chickpeas, 39, 48, 50, 69, 73, 75, 134, 136
Chokha, 136
Chora, 51, 69, 71, 136
Chori, 136
Chutney, 8, 10, 16, 28, 33, 37, 41, 43-45, 53-54, 69, 100, 133
Cinnamon, 22, 29, 33, 63, 77, 81, 87, 91, 103, 125, 113, 135, 137
Cloves, 22-23, 44-45, 52-53, 87, 89, 91-93, 113, 134, 136
Cob, 67
Cobi, 57-58, 61, 136
Coconut, 16, 35-37, 41, 43, 50, 52, 83, 116, 119, 125, 137
Coffee, 127
Colic, 88, 94, 134-135
Colocassia, 137
Constipation, 134-135
Corn, 67, 137
Coughs, 46, 113, 126, 134-135
Courgettes, 30, 67
Cucumber, 105, 108, 134, 137
Curd, 120

D

Dahi, 41, 47, 51, 136
Dates, 13, 34, 41, 44
Dhana, 136
Dhania, 13, 31, 94, 134
Dhanna-jeeru, 22-23
Dhokhra, 27, 35, 96, 136
Dhosa, 16, 43, 47, 52-53, 136
Dill, 22, 92, 135, 137
Diwali, 11

Dough, 33-34, 117
Drumstick, 137
Dudhi, 136
Dumplings, 51, 136-137

E

Elaychi, 134, 136
Elchi, 22-23

F

Fennel, 36, 108, 125, 125, 135
Fenugreek, 22-23, 30, 60, 67, 75,
100-101, 105, 112, 135, 137
Fibres, 44, 49, 57
Flu, 92, 127, 131
Fritters, 20, 30, 47, 69, 136
Fruit, 10, 41, 105, 116, 120
Fudge, 116, 136
Fudna-wari, 127, 131

G

Gajjar, 115, 119, 136
Garam-Masala, 22-23, 60, 63, 69,
71-73, 75-77, 83
Giloda, 67
Glossary, 136-137
Gooseberry, 112
Gor, 105, 136
Gourd, 104, 134, 136-137
Greenbeans, 57, 59
Griddle, 52-53, 137
Gulab, 115, 117, 136
Guwar, 67, 136

H

Haat, 78
Halwa, 115, 119, 136
Hardar, 22, 52, 92, 93, 134, 136
Haricot, 72

Herbs, 22, 132
Hindu, 9-11, 13
Hing, 52, 72, 88, 93, 134, 136
Holistic, 13
Honey, 128
Husk, 78

I

Ice-cream, 119
Idli, 41 136
Iron, 60, 100, 135

J

Jaggery, 105, 136
Jaifer, 134
Jalebis, 115
Jambu, 115, 117, 136
Jaundice, 135
Jeeru, 22, 94, 134, 136
Juwar, 136

K

Kabuli, 50
Kachori, 27, 33, 136
Kachumbar, 105
Kadhi, 17, 23, 60, 63, 78-79, 81, 83,
87, 89, 92, 136
Kadi-patta, 134
Kaju, 136
Kakadi, 134
Kakira, 8
Kanda, 136
Karai, 20, 27, 101
Karela, 104, 134, 136
Kathor, 69, 71-73, 75-77
Kenya, 11, 57
Keri, 136
Keri-no-chundo, 105, 113
Keri-no-raas, 116
Kesar, 136
Ketchup, 10, 43-44, 105, 109, 133

Kheers, 115-116, 136
Khichadi, 60, 63, 79, 89, 136
Kidney, 69, 91,137, 134-135
Koftas, 67, 136

L

Lactation, 134
Ladle, 52
Ladoos, 115-116
Lapsi, 23, 115-116, 125, 136
Lassi, 127-129, 136
Lassun, 46, 134, 136
Laving, 22-23, 134, 136
Leftovers, 27, 59, 83, 105, 132-133
Lentil, 136-137
Lettuce, 105-106, 111
Lila-marcha, 136
Lili-hardar, 136
Limdi, 35, 43, 92, 136
Limdo, 134
Lime, 106
Long-grain, 78

M

Maag, 51, 69, 76, 135-136
Maag-ni-daal, 137
Magaj, 96
Maharashtra, 11
Makai-no-chevdo, 27, 39
Makai, 137
Malai, 137
Mamra, 137
Mandarins, 120
Mange, 67
Mango, 105, 112-113, 116, 127,
129, 136
Maragi, 79, 91
Marcha, 40, 136-137
Marcha-ni-bhukhi, 22
Mari, 136
Mari-masala, 22-23
Masala-wari, 127, 131
Mash, 44

Malai, 137
Mamra, 137
Mandarins, 120
Mange, 67
Mango, 105, 112-113, 116, 127, 129, 136
Maragi, 79, 91
Marcha, 40, 136-137
Marcha-ni-bhukhi, 22
Mari, 136
Mari-masala, 22-23
Masala-wari, 127, 131
Mash, 44
Masoor, 137
Mattar, 135, 137
Mathya, 96
Mattar, 57, 61, 65
Measurements, 18, 132
Medicinal, 78, 134-135
Mendo, 137
Methi, 22-23, 135, 137
Methi-ni-bhaji, 137
Metric, 18
Millet, 136
Mint, 10, 29, 41, 43, 45, 127, 131
Mochi, 9
Muli, 105, 135
Mung, 33, 69, 76, 89, 135-137
Mura, 105
Muro, 135
Muslin, 120
Muth, 137
Muthiya, 69, 75

N

Naan, 95, 101
Nariyal, 137
Nashto, 27
Nimakh, 22, 137
Noodles, 137
Nutmeg, 134
Nutrients, 57, 78, 135
Nuts, 41, 83, 87, 116, 120, 123, 136-137

O

Okra, 136
Olive, 18
Ondhiyu, 57, 67
Ondhwo, 47, 54, 96
Oregano, 132

P

Palak, 135
Palm, 51
Pancake, 16, 52-53, 96, 100, 136
Paneer, 137
Pani, 47-49, 137
Papad, 96, 137
Papadom, 96, 137
Paretha, 95, 102-103, 105, 137
Patlo, 21
Patra, 27, 36-37, 137
Patta, 134-135
Pau, 10, 27, 29
Peanuts, 29, 36, 41, 45, 50, 63, 67
Peas, 33-34, 49-50, 52, 57-58, 61, 65, 67, 81, 86, 93, 135-137
Pepper, 83, 86, 91, 105, 108, 111, 136
Petis, 27, 34
Pickle, 105, 112
Pilau, 79, 81, 83, 85, 92, 137
Pistachio, 116, 119-120, 122, 123, 125, 137
Posho, 57, 59
Preserve, 105, 113
Proteins, 11, 68, 135
Puda, 95, 100
Puffed, 49
Pulp, 49, 134
Pulses, 8, 13, 21-23, 69, 136
Puran, 95
Puris, 20-21, 47-49, 58, 95, 98, 105, 113, 137
Puwa, 137

R

Radishes, 105-106, 135
Ragdo, 137
Rai, 26, 135, 137
Raitas, 22, 105-106, 108-109, 111-113, 137
Rajma, 135, 137
Ravaiya, 57, 63, 137
Rice, 22-23, 27, 34-35
Ringan, 56-57, 65, 134, 137
Root, 10, 131
Rotla, 95
Rotli, 63, 95, 97, 105, 132-133, 137

S

Saansi, 20
Saffron, 117, 123, 136
Salad, 8, 69,, 83, 91, 105-106, 108-109, 111-113, 132-133
Sambhar, 16, 52-53, 137
Sambharo, 105, 111
Seasoning, 105
Seeded, 86
Seero, 115-116, 123, 137
Semolina, 48, 100, 115-117, 123, 137
Seragwo, 137
Sesame, 29, 35-37, 54, 67, 137
Sev, 23, 39, 115-116, 122, 137
Shak, 57, 137
Shirkand, 115, 116, 120, 137
Soji, 137
Soy, 86
Soya, 69
Spice-tin, 20, 22
Spices, 20, 22-23
Spinach, 57, 60, 79, 87, 135-136
Sprouts, 69
Starch, 78
Starters, 8, 16, 44, 47, 54
Steam, 21
Sukha, 22
Sultanas, 33, 116, 119, 122-123, 125

Sunflower, 18
Suwa, 135, 137
Swahili, 8
Sweet, 41, 44, 49, 67, 96, 105, 115-116, 127-128
Sweetcorn, 29, 39, 54, 57, 59, 79, 81, 86-87
Syrup, 113, 117, 136

T

Taj, 22-23, 135, 137
Tal, 137
Tamarind, 34, 37, 41, 44, 48-49, 134, 136
Tameta, 137
Tanzania, 11
Tapelas, 21
Tava, 20
Tavi, 20, 137
Tea, 23, 27, 97, 127, 131, 136
Thali, 137
Tikhi, 95, 98
Tikka, 10
Toast, 83
Toasties, 44, 45, 59, 64, 73, 133
Tongs, 20
Tonic, 135
Tooth, 115
Traditional, 57, 67
Turmeric, 22-23, 35-36
Turya, 137
Tuwer, 52, 53, 93, 137
Tuwer-ni-sing, 137

U

Uganda, 8, 11, 14
Urad, 52, 96, 135 137
Utensils, 20-21, 27

V

Vaal, 23, 69, 72
Vada, 41, 47, 51, 136-137
Valor, 67, 137
Variyari, 135
Vedas, 13
Vegan, 23
Velan, 21
Vermicelli, 39, 115-116, 122, 137
Vitamins, 11, 57, 68,

W

Waghaar, 23
Wheat, 36, 95, 98, 102, 115-116, 125, 136
Wholemeal, 95
Wok, 27, 30, 86, 101, 111